AF817759

GEO. W. TRENDLE

GEO. W. TRENDLE

CREATOR AND PRODUCER OF

The Lone Ranger
The Green Hornet
Sgt. Preston of the Yukon
The American Agent
And Other Successes

An Authorized Biography by

Mary E. Bickel

An Exposition-Banner Book
Exposition Press New York

EXPOSITION PRESS INC.

50 Jericho Turnpike Jericho, New York 11753

FIRST EDITION

© 1971 by Mary E. Bickel. *All rights reserved, including the right of reproduction in whole or in part in any form except for short quotations in critical essays and reviews.* Manufactured in the United States of America.

LIBRARY OF CONGRESS CATALOG CARD NUMBER: 79-171704

0-682-47348-0

Preface

It was an exciting, fascinating experience, this reminiscing with the subject of this biography.

Born in the 1880's, he lived through the most fantastic era in all entertainment history. It was a privilege to accompany him as he went back in memory.

With no knowledge of the English language, this son of a German emigrant family entered an Ohio primary school at the age of five and began to earn money when he was six. He worked his way through college to get his law degree and became a millionaire in his early thirties. "How to Become a Millionaire While Pursuing an Ideal" might easily be the title of this book.

From the days of the St. Louis Fair, through the days of the penny arcade, through the days when an old store building with stiff wooden chairs set in rows was called a theatre, through silent pictures where one watched heroes with lipstick perform superhuman deeds and when the music came from a pit directly under the screen where the pianist improvised an accompaniment to fit the action over his head—from all this pioneering and experimenting we went on to the addition of sound and eventually color!

Then came the marvel of radio sound waves carrying entertainment right into the home; and then, wonder of wonders, television, when pictures joined sound—in black and white at first and then also in color.

We saw, on our trip back in time, the greats of the entertainment field in the days of their beginnings—Bob Hope,

Eddie Cantor, Al Jolson, Fannie Brice, Will Rogers, W. C. Fields, Mary Pickford, Douglas Fairbanks, Charles Chaplin and many others who achieved leadership in their way as our subject did in his.

Occasionally he would chuckle, remembering some amusing incident. Then again, he would have to be prodded because he has a certain shyness, a reluctance to talk about himself.

After having gathered the factual material for this biography, and feeling a responsibility to entertain the reader, I might have been tempted to add to or subtract from the facts to increase interest. But I realized that the facts, as told to me, are in themselves so fantastic as to make such embroidery of truth unnecessary.

The data were gathered—the little and big happenings, the dreams and aspirations—and put together in this book to share with you.

m. e. b.

I

Across the fields of yesterday
He sometimes comes to me,
A little lad just back from play—
The lad I used to be.
THOMAS SAMUEL JONES, JR., *Sometimes*

HE CAME UP THE STEPS of the back porch, step by step, his small body swaying from right to left, and left to right, with each step. He was four years old.

Baking day, he realized, and he savored the wonderful odor of brown sugar, cinnamon, butter and vanilla all mixed together. It was really a special baking day, for tomorrow was his birthday, and the evidence of that was the huge, deep rich chocolate cake, decorated with thick and luscious frosting.

Here in his mother's kitchen was love and understanding. Here he could come when he was hungry; there was always some sweet something produced to appease his hunger. Here he could come when the neighborhood children, with typical childish cruelty, ridiculed his thick German accent or his lack of comprehension.

His mother would be at her sewing machine more often than not, both feet on the treadle, her body bent slightly toward the needle. The machine would sing—a lovely song of accomplishment because most of the clothing in this house was put together at that machine.

He would walk around to the back of the machine so that he could see her face. Soon she would look up. He would wait. Sometimes she would just smile, and sometimes she would smile and wink as if they shared a great secret; but today she straightened up and closed both eyes in a sort of double wink, crinkling her whole face in a welcome. Then, as usual, she extended her right arm. He moved around the sewing machine to be in the circle of that arm—safe and secure. Here he was wanted; here he was a person who mattered; here he was important.

Tomorrow was his birthday, and tomorrow, as she did on every birthday, she would repeat the story of his birth, as if it were the most important birth in this household, and he would experience the warm wonderful feeling that he was a very special fellow. All of his later life he would recall the details of his mother's story. In manhood, when loneliness or unhappiness overtook him, he would recall and take comfort from the recollection. Then, in his imagination, he could smell the familiar baking odors—sugar, cinnamon, butter, vanilla; he could feel his mother's arm around his shoulders; then, for a moment, all was right, and it was a good world again.

It was a very good world the next morning too, for this was July Fourth, 1889, and he was five years old. Already people were celebrating his birthday—firecrackers in the distance, shouts from one house to the other. He climbed out of bed, dressed quickly and down the stairs into the kitchen just as the oven door was opened, and out came the *kaffee kuchen.*

"Sit down, George," said his mother. He wriggled in anticipation. "This is your birthday—just five years ago you came."

The little boy looked up. "You knew I was coming," he prompted.

"We all knew you were coming. We had picked your name."

"What was my name to be? Tell me." He had heard the story before, but he didn't want to miss a single detail. It went something like this:

The large building on Foster Avenue in Norwalk, Ohio, housed both business and residence–side by side, with a common partition, so that if one were on the residence side of the building, Peter Trendle could hear the tinkle of the bell, which rang over the front door of the store, when customers arrived. Often a dinner or a lunch would be interrupted a couple of times, and the proprietor would get impatient. There was always the awareness of a possibility, and one listened as one ate.

This day was July Fourth, in the year 1884. The father had been down in the cellar of the store, bottling vinegar from the huge cask which stood beside the cider and the wine casks. The listening habit was strong–he could hear his wife's footsteps as she walked back and forth in the kitchen. "Her step is heavier," he thought, and decided to leave the bottling for the time and go upstairs. Anyway, he was hot and dusty.

As usual he went directly to the kitchen sink, primed the water pump from a pail standing there and half filled the large pan for washing. Without a word the woman picked up the large dipper at the back of the stove, opened the warm-water reservoir, filled the tin dipper and carried it to the sink and poured it into the basin.

Through the soap he shouted, "Enough!"

No answer came to him. He turned quickly and saw his wife, dead white, bent over the table.

"Get the doctor," she said.

"But I talked to him yesterday, and he said it would be two or three days at least."

"It is now!"

"The doctor is at the Fourth of July picnic."

"Get him–get him now. Drop the girls off at Liz's and tell her to come."

He ran out of the house, his shirttails flying, grabbed the

three little girls from the back yard and pushed them into the grocery cart which stood behind the house. He harnessed the horse in a daze and took off for the picnic grounds without explaining to the girls, who had no idea what was giving them this unexpected pleasure. Rides at this speed were rare, and they hung on for their lives.

At the picnic ground, with people milling around, he didn't see the doctor at once. "Girls, split up, find the doctor and get back here."

The ride back was even more exciting for the girls because then there were five in the seat, all excited but the doctor, who remarked, "A little early, eh?"

The driver showed no inclination for small talk, and anyway, who could talk above the squeals and screeches of the little girls?

The doctor was deposited on the front porch, and the man remembered to deliver the girls to their aunt's house–three doors from their own house–giving her the message to come at once. "In a moment," she said, "I'll walk over."

His dinner was still on the back of the stove, covered and keeping warm, where, between pains, his wife had placed it. He toyed with the idea of filling his plate, but he lacked appetite now. He went to the stairs just as the doctor put his head out of the bedroom.

"Where is the nurse?"

"Coming."

"All right. Send her in as soon as she comes–and you take a walk. We don't need you right now."

Out on the porch, in the swing, he noted it creaked. "I'll oil that in the morning," he thought. It was indeed the only sound in that stillness, and it bothered him so that he rose to go into the store to get the oilcan, when up the street came Aunt Liz, her long skirts held at one side but still hitting the road a bit so that she seemed to be riding on a cloud of dust. Up the steps and around the man without once glancing at him, she went inside.

Silently he hooted to himself, "She doesn't like me any more than I like her. But there is a woman who makes things hum. We'll have a happening soon. She is the general leading the troops." He was caught out of the present for the moment, but soon he put out his hand to still the creak of the swing as he left it. Cupping his hand over his eyes, he peered through the kitchen window; seeing nothing, he tiptoed to the edge of the porch and sat on the top step.

Everything was still in a quiet which held him like a vise. He started at every little sound; a pan moved across the stove inside; a step on the stair inside. Once in a while a firecracker went off in the distance, and he would be startled. A neighbor called out, "Fine day." He didn't answer–just waved his hand.

Suddenly the stillness was broken–was cracked wide open –for the dinner period had passed at the picnic, and the firecrackers, forbidden before lunch, were being shot off. Children pounded on tins–anything to make noise–and in the midst of this din the doctor tapped the man on the shoulder and announced, "It's a boy."

"Ja, sure, it's a boy," said the man, "what else?" and realizing what he had been waiting for, he asked, "he didn't cry. Is he all right?"

In an attempt at levity the doctor said, "No, he didn't cry; he just made a fist and shook it at me. Yes, he's all right; he's fine."

The father nodded.

"Your wife says you will name him William; is that so?"

"We agreed–yes," said the father.

Just then an unusually loud firecracker burst, and the father said, "But born on the Fourth of July? He will be George Washington–George Washington Trendle." He repeated, "George Washington Trendle," and decided the sound was just right.

"Get me back to that picnic," said the doctor, and the man answered, "You bet," as he jumped into the wagon again.

II

THE BLANK SPACES ON THE BIRTH CERTIFICATE were filled in: "George Washington Trendle," born July 4, 1884; mother Pauline Trendle, born Germany; father Peter Trendle, born Germany. Other information regarding his parents came to George from them.

His father, Peter Trendle, was born July 25, 1852, in a small town in Germany–Waldshut. When he was nineteen, he migrated to America and settled for a time in Sandusky, Ohio. No one recorded the reason for his settling there. But here he met and married Pauline Seufert, who was born in Karlshrue, Germany, on October 24, 1855. Pauline came to America, also to Sandusky, when she was eleven. There was quite a large German colony in Sandusky. After marriage, Pauline and Peter moved to Norwalk, Ohio, where they found another German colony. It was perfectly natural for them to continue to communicate in their native tongue.

So it happened that in the house on Foster Avenue in Norwalk, to which the couple moved early in their marriage, no English was spoken. Although his older sisters had learned the new language in school, there was no way for George to learn, and he entered school at the age of five with a tremendous handicap: he didn't know a word of English! But he did have an interpreter, Albert Hund.

Albert was his cousin. They were both five years old, and they had a wonderful understanding. They told each other of their dreams. "I am going to be a minister," said George.

"I'll be a businessman," said Albert. "Why would you want to be a minister?"

And George couldn't phrase the ambition, so he would

go on. "Remember when we had a big fire at our house, Albert? In the middle of the night when the house and the store burned down, my father carried me out in my nightshirt. We all stood there and watched the house burn down. Then we all went to live with you and Aunt Liz until our new house was built. Wasn't that fun?"

Albert would nod. "What an experience!" he would think.

In the fall both entered the Norwalk school. The seating was arranged alphabetically, and George sat ahead of Albert by three rows. When the teacher looked directly at George and talked, he would turn around in his seat. "P-s-s-t."

Albert would look up.

"*Was hat sie gesagt?*" George would ask.

And the teacher, wanting to teach George the language, would caution both boys. George, not understanding, would insist to Albert that he tell him what the teacher had said and would become impatient:

"*Sie hat gesagt–*" began the boy.

"Albert," said the teacher, "you will stop talking."

The first grade–there were no kindergartens in those days –was difficult enough without a language barrier. Your mother is at home, your friend is three seats behind you, and it is forbidden to ask him for help! You are given impossible tasks by a large woman in a room surrounded by strangers who giggle at your discomfiture and mimic your German accent! George was unhappy. But he stood it for two weeks; and then on a cold day, during recess, he decided he had had enough.

He waited until the children had all gone back into the building and then climbed the picket fence which surrounded the school yard. One foot over the top of the fence, he found it was too high. He would have to go out the front gate; so he swung his leg back down and in doing so, caught his pants on the point of the picket.

Albert, missing his cousin, came running back, and the teacher came right out after Albert. There was George, inside the fence, his pants torn up the back to the waist. Back in the classroom, while she sent for his sister in a higher grade, the teacher stood George in front of her desk, his back to the pupils, to their utter delight, for the two pieces of his pants were apart and his little rear was entirely exposed. The children could not contain themselves–they giggled and tittered. The room was in an uproar.

George was mortified with a humiliation which he never forgot. It was a cruel lesson to a small boy. Years later he could hear the children titter and remember how, for months afterward, they would point at his pants and cross their fingers in the old "shame" gesture. He grew to loathe ridicule in any form. Even as a man he would go to any length to avoid the possibility of ridicule for himself or anyone else.

At the supper table that night George announced, "I am never going back to that school." His sister had just completed her account of the afternoon's experience.

"But you must," she said. "You must have an education to be anything."

"What's the use?" he asked. "I can't read, I can't write. I don't know what they are saying, the teacher won't let me talk, and the kids make fun of me." He was bursting with indignation. No one laughed.

His mother looked across the table to her husband. He nodded, and then he said, "From now on only English will be spoken in this house. You girls help George." It was, and they did.

And George was on his way!

Summer came and with it vacation from school. George took his first job. The J. L. Hudson Company, which had a branch in Norwalk, hired him and his cousin Albert to deliver handbills on Saturday afternoons. At the end of the first afternoon, when they had carefully folded the handbills and placed one between every doorknob and door jamb, they returned to the store to report. They were given the unbelievable sum of fifty cents each for their labor! The boys were dazzled by their sudden riches. They decided to keep it a secret, except from their mothers. Nevertheless, in a few weeks, George's father learned of the new job.

"George, I hear you are a big boy now; you have a job!"

George nodded.

"I too have a new job. I am adding washing machines to my business. Now you can work for your own father. I will have the leaflets printed, and you will distribute them for me."

While the prospect did not elate them, both boys said, "Yes."

The following Saturday, having worked as assiduously as they had for Hudson's, the boys reported back. The man handed each of the boys three pennies.

"But," said George, "Hudson's give us fifty cents."

"So," said the father, "you are not working for Hudson's now—you are working for me."

The following Saturday, Albert went back to work for Hudson's. George took his father's handbills, and that day and each Saturday thereafter he deposited them under a bridge that ran over a creek several blocks from their home. He didn't ask for any pay from his father, and he was offered none. But since the handbills had brought no business, the father decided to discontinue them after a few weeks—and George went back to work for the Hudson store.

Sometimes the boys "skinny-dipped" in the creek at the wooded area. Although it was forbidden to swim in the creek, there never was any comment when he came home shiny clean and with his hair smoothed down.

More often they went to the granary, near the old railroad tracks, where the farmers brought in their wheat and oats and where these were stored until shipping capacity was reached.

A series of buckets on a chain picked up the grain and carried it on up to be dumped into the bins. These were ten feet square and about twenty feet deep. A ladder on the inside met the outside ladder at the top. At the back of the granary a blind horse was tied to a horizontal pole about fifteen feet long and geared so that the horse walked in a circle. This turned the center pole and moved the buckets which carried the grain up. Round and round and round the old horse went, and at first this furnished some fascination for the boys. But they soon found another and more dangerous fascination.

They climbed up the ladder on the outside of the bin and lowered themselves down on the inside just as the buckets began to move. The delicious feel of the grain pouring down their backs was so entrancing that it brought them back day after day.

Sundays and holidays were just great! His father was a leader in the Democratic party in Norwalk. George would stand on the sidewalk and watch the parade go by. His father, resplendent in his light-gray high plug hat, cutaway coat and polished shoes, marched at the head of the parade. Sometimes there were evening parades, and the torch lights were held high as they marched right down the main street of Norwalk. It was a grand sight!

It was the year 1891, and soon it would be election time. The business, a small luncheon-bar, which Peter Trendle had founded when the grocery store burned down, was in a new area and needed much help to build up. German potato salad, baked beans and other baked goods were made at home, and

George would remember later on that he would carry these to the luncheon-bar. Times were so poor that the business was very slow in establishing itself.

And then came the election. Formerly Democratic, the entire town overwhelmingly went Republican. Peter Trendle was a bitter man as he opened his business the following day.

"You had to expect this change," said his first customer.

"Ach"—and he pushed his hands away from himself in a gesture of disgust.

"Times have been very bad. Everyone has felt that a change is needed. I myself voted Republican."

This was too much for Peter. "Out!" he shouted. "Get out, you turncoat!"

The man rose, protesting, but he left. The scene was repeated over and over, with variations. The man's disposition simply curdled. He felt it a personal affront that many of his former friends had turned away from "the party." Most of them had been customers. He grumbled or scolded or waited on them with such surliness that soon they stayed away, and the business became a dismal failure. The home was foreclosed, the horse was taken, and Peter was forced to look for greener pastures.

He left Norwalk for Detroit, alone.

III

Jobs were scarce in 1891. The country was leaning toward the panic of 1893. And a man with little business experience found the going hard. The stores, themselves in trouble, would hire no new people. Peter Trendle looked elsewhere, and finally, discouraged, took a job driving a horsecar on Gratiot Avenue in Detroit.

He sent for his family. With their few remaining possessions they moved by wagon to Sandusky and thence by boat to Detroit. For seven-year-old George it was a wondrous experience.

His father was not so happy. Accustomed to running his own business, he found it hard to take orders. The horsecars in 1891 were exactly as in the later cartoons. Two horses were hitched to the front of the car. Directly behind them, unprotected from the weather, sat the driver. At the end of the run the horses were unhitched and placed at the other end of the car, where another driver's seat was installed.

The passengers fared much better. Inside the car hay was spread on the floor, protecting the passengers' feet from the cold. Open windows kept the passengers cool in the summer while the roof protected them from the sun. The driver had no such conveniences.

On Jefferson Avenue in Detroit the ladies from nearby Grosse Pointe would leave their own horses and carriages to be driven home, board the horsecar at the end of the line and go to downtown Detroit for a day of shopping. In the evenings their husbands would drive them home.

In the meantime the rides to the downtown area were social events! Ideas were exchanged, gossip was repeated, and as often as not, in the summer, when the windows were opened, the driver was included in the discussions. It was considered quite proper and indeed an advantage to know the driver by his first name. In this one field of American endeavor there was little if any snobbery.

Peter Trendle worked on the Gratiot line, and there was no socializing with the passengers. Still, he seemed comparatively content until:

The wheels of the horsecar were centered, and it was easy to rock the car forward and back if enough people boarded at the back at the same time. A group of young men, smart-alecks, grouped themselves on the back platform and began to rock the car. Ultimately the car would have been in trouble, but the driver didn't wait for such an eventuality. He stopped his horses and started to the back of the car, intent on stopping the horseplay, when a sudden lurch sent the horses into action. The six young men and the driver were thrown from the car. Running after his car, to the tune of screaming female passengers, and while he caught his horses, the driver marched into the office at the close of the day and quit! He went to work as night watchman in the Banner Laundry.

George was seven when he entered Norvell School in Detroit. Hazen S. Pingree was the mayor of Detroit, a city of 205,876 population. The Union Guardian Trust Company was founded that same year, as was the McGregor Institute.

This was before the days of intelligence-quotient tests. In order to be on the safe side, a pupil who arrived from a different school was automatically put back one grade, a serious blow to a young man's pride. So George employed his time in small mischiefs, little nuisances, until Christmas time, when the school play was being planned. A duet with a *girl* was planned for George, and he openly rebelled. So vociferous was his objection that the teacher and principal decided to move him to a higher grade, where he must work harder. "Nuisance value" was a phrase that he was to learn in later years, but he really had it right then!

In his fifth grade, after a hassle with the teacher over putting snowballs down a girl's neck, he was again moved to a higher grade. He was thirteen when he was graduated class president and valedictorian.

He wrote in his valedictory address, "Today we are still together, but in a few years, all will be changed. No more shall we be together in this world but we hope we shall meet in another world." It was June 24, 1899, and he was still dreaming of the pulpit.

George and his new friends found their way to Belle Isle and the bathhouse. They crossed the Belle Isle bridge, entered the gates into the bathhouse and swam in the Detroit River. Drying off later was quite a procedure. Hanging from the rafters on a large spool-like bar was a giant roller towel. The boys would jump on the towel, ride it for a moment, then swing about in monkey-like acrobatics. All of this was done with an eye on the clock, for the first thirty minutes of swimming and bathing were free to boys under fifteen. Swimming in the river was *verboten* too, but if his slicked-down hair and shiny clean face were noticed at home, it was never mentioned.

This vacation period was spent in a different atmosphere. For with the breadwinner's new job, the family was moved from the East Side of Detroit to the North Side on Brady Street, where a small house was purchased.

One morning his father stopped him and asked, "When will you begin to work, George? You're a big boy now."

"I want to go to college, so I have to go to high school."

"College, high school–what do you want with that?"

"I just want to be somebody."

"You are big enough to be somebody now–somebody who helps keep this house going."

George's face turned red. "I am going to get a college education, Dad, someway, somehow."

"Then you figure the 'someway, somehow.' This much I will give: If you want to take a commercial course in high school and learn bookkeeping, all right, but the Latin, the biology, that is out."

"But, Dad–"

"Take it or leave it."

George took it. He began high school in the fall. He was taking a business course, but his goal, a college degree, seemed farther and farther away. He delivered daily papers for the Detroit *Journal* at $5 a month, plus what he could make by added sales.

The first year dragged, and the boy was discouraged. At this point his three sisters decided they would provide the tuition for an intensive stenographic course. All older than George, they had each received this education and were all working and of course contributing to the expense of the household. George accepted, and completed the six-month course in five months. He was fifteen years old and had been earning money for ten years!

The Newsboys' Association, to which most of the paper carriers belonged, met every Sunday evening in the Shoe Company Building on Jefferson Avenue. Dues were ten cents a week. George pail no dues for the reason that he had taken up playing the harmonica and sat on the platform with the mandolin-guitar group and played for the meeting. Every Christmas, Russell Alger gave each boy a new suit of clothes, while the Shoe Company gave each a pair of new shoes.

George's father in the meantime had become a sort of night engineer at the Banner Laundry. He had gotten a raise, but his was still a small salary even in those days, and he also had the idea that children should contribute to the household as soon as they were able. He had bought the old house on

Brady Street. He made the payments, paid the taxes and maintained the building with repairs and additions, but the girls, Jennie, Minnie and Clara, put George through the five-month business-school course and bought food and clothing for themselves and their mother. George bought his own. One afternoon George had a conversation with his mother which went like this:

"Mother, do you think I am wasting my time? Do you think I should go out and get some kind of a job which doesn't take a college education?"

"You still want college, George?"

"Mother, I want to be somebody–I want to be able to do more for you and the girls. I can't do it unless I get a better education than I have."

"Then get it!"

IV

The Lake Salt Company on the dock at the foot of Randolph Street in Detroit hired young George Trendle, fresh out of business college, to work as their stenographer, bookkeeper, clerk, salesman and collector. But George neglected one very important factor in his negotiation: he forgot to mention salary. When he did remember, he was too shy to ask. It was a full month before salary was mentioned at all, and the boy had to ask the employer for his salary. He was paid the munificent sum of $5 a week!

His father hit the ceiling. He demanded that George ask for more money.

"What if they won't give it to me?"

"Then you quit and get another job."

Here his mother broke her long-time rule of no interference, and said, "No, you will stay there until you do get a raise. Not until then may you quit."

It was almost a full year before George worked up enough courage to ask for a raise.

"Do you think I am worth more than five dollars a week?" he asked his employer one morning.

"Why, yes," came the surprising answer, "I guess you are. Well, now, from here on you'll be getting ten dollars a week."

"No," said the boy, "I think I have been worth ten dollars a week for almost a year. So I quit."

Jones and Laughlin Steel Company hired George Trendle at fifteen dollars a week. There were three young men and one woman in the office. The boys were all about the same age and inclined more than a little to horseplay. The woman was a Miss Behan who had little patience with the young men and their antics. But she liked George, who was quite serious about his work. The boys noted this and decided to play a joke. It took this form:

They called George into the vault one day, held his hands and pulled off his trousers, taking them out of the vault with them and leaving George in his "lowers" only. Then they asked Miss Behan to step into the vault, saying George had a question.

When she saw his condition. she screamed, ran into her own office and locked the door. The boys hooted with laughter. George was furious and within himself vowed vengeance. It wasn't long in coming.

The assistant manager had been given a box of cigars–twenty-five cent cigars at that–and after taking out a handful, left the box in his office.

The boys, except for George, smoked cigars and congratulated themselves on this find. Each took a cigar, on the theory that the owner would not miss one. And each continued taking one, every day or two, on the same theory but not knowing that the other boys were also swiping cigars. Paul Billings, one of the boys, even told George what good cigars they were.

The owner of the box opened it a couple of weeks later, and finding four cigars left, sent for the boys, one by one. George came first. "You know I don't smoke," he said, "but if you want the real picture, why don't you call the boys in one at a time?" The boys came in one at a time; each admitted he thought the assistant manager was smoking the cigars, and each was given a dressing down. As they came out of the office George winked and laughed. The prank involving Miss Behan was avenged–George was no longer the "new boy."

About this time Jones and Laughlin opened a branch office in St. Louis. George was offered a job with the company there and the salary would be $75 a month, a fine incentive for further advancement, so he accepted at once. His co-workers and friends gave a farewell dinner party in his honor. Robert H. Flowerday was the toastmaster, according to the small red programs for the affair, and there was music and speeches. The date was October 3, 1902, and George was eighteen years old.

Of his $75, he sent $20 to his mother and lived on the other $55. His quarters were one small partitioned space at the end of the hall on the second floor of a boardinghouse. There was barely room to turn around in; the closet was a curtained space in the corner with a shelf at the top. For this, plus his board, George paid the sum of $5 a week. At the same time he began a lifetime habit of regular savings. There were various ways, and he found most of them.

Mennen's Borated Talcum Toilet Powder advertised "Get Mennen's, only a little higher in price than worthless substitutes. Sold everywhere for twenty-five cents." The manufacturer would have been surprised to learn its other uses. The can was round with a cover that was also rounded, and it fitted perfectly into the toe or heel of a sock. The boys would organize a mending evening. They sat around offering each other suggestions and criticisms. There was some joking, but they were dead serious about this accomplishment.

In later years, when George recounted this experience, someone asked, "What did you do when the cans were changed to square cans?" He answered very quickly, "By that time I didn't have to mend socks."

The job at Jones and Laughlin was to come to an abrupt close. St. Louis in the summer can be hot, and in the year 1902 there was no air conditioning, so the employees made frequent trips to the washbowl to wash hands or dampen neck and brow with towels.

One hot afternoon the office was deserted, except for George and a young office clerk, female. After many trips to the washbowl, one of them brought back the wet towel and flicked it at the other playfully. Next a game was worked out —each, armed with a towel, straddled the railing which separated the office desks from the reception area and began the flicking, when the door suddenly opened. The office manager walked in, and both were fired on the spot.

The firing developed into an advantage, for George went to work for the Ralston Purina Company at more pay.

George's predecessor at Ralston had left the books in a completely confused condition. They had not been balanced for six months. There was no time for horseplay here. George worked long hours at no extra pay to straighten out the books.

"Dear George," began the letter from his sister Jen, "Mother is coming to surprise you. She is lonely and so are we. Father is just the same as ever. I wish you were here."

He had barely read the letter, when his mother walked into the boardinghouse. She stayed for two days, during which she urged her boy to come home, generally mothered the group of friends to whom he had attached himself, mended George's clothes, added some more and left with the promise that if a suitable job could be found for him, George would return to Detroit, resume his studies and live at home.

It was the year 1904, when the St. Louis Fair had closed —or as it was called in St. Louis, the Louisiana Purchase Exposition. The Winton Motor Carriage Company had advertised that their Winton Motor Phaeton had made the run from Cleveland to New York in forty-eight actual running hours at an average speed of fifteen miles an hour! The Carpenter Electric of 1895 vintage led the way for the Stanley Steamer, the Starin, the Buffalo Electric and the Sandusky and preceded the Waverly, the Lancanmobile and the Columbia Oldsmobile. Advertised as the "Boss of the Road" by the

Ford Motor Company of 691 Mack Avenue in Detroit, was the "latest and the best Fordmobile with a detachable tonneau," for the sum of $850.

In Detroit, Jennie, George's eldest sister, was secretary to the manager of the L. C. Smith Typewriter Company, and when the president of the Caille Brothers Company bought a typewriter and mentioned casually to the manager that he was looking for a purchasing agent, she saw her opportunity to provide work for her brother and get him back to his home in Detroit. The job promise brought him home.

George was interviewed for the job, and he gave an honest appraisal of his past experience, adding just enough to make the president of Caille Brothers feel that he was getting an outstanding young man for the job.

Caille Brothers made slot machines, gum machines and candy machines, as well as a myriad of gambling devices. They had their own woodworking and casting departments. It would be George's job to buy, at an advantage, tools, files, drills, lumber, paint, varnish and other materials.

He knew little or nothing about these things or their prices, but he was eager and willing to work to learn. The factory manager recognized this on George's first morning.

"I know you don't know a damned thing about this stuff," was his greeting on his first working day.

George nodded.

"Well," said the factory manager, Dick Kraetke, "you stick with me, keep your mouth shut, and I'll help you work this thing out."

True to his word, he made a list of materials necessary for each day's work. George took the list and went to the stockroom, where he found and studied each piece, how it was used and how much was needed. Then he studied the records to learn prices. He did the job so well that he was later moved to the main office.

George had established himself! He enrolled in the night classes of the Detroit College of Law. Somewhere he had lost his ambition to be a minister. When he thought about it, he felt sure that he could be more useful as a lawyer, and he worked to that end. Between his job and his studies there was little time left for social activity.

Occasionally he would take out a pretty young file clerk from the Caille Brothers office. She was Kathryn M. Mylne and destined to become more important in George's life. At that time, however, nothing was farther from George's mind than marriage. His eye was on that precious law degree.

George discovered that while he might obtain his degree, he could not be admitted to the bar without certain of the high-school credits he had missed. These credits had to be earned evenings during the summer months at Y.M.C.A. night school while he continued his law classes in the winter months.

He held no class office, but he was graduated four years later with a percentage mark of 95, one of five in the class! And he rented an office in the Moffett Building with his school chum, Edmond J. Stafford, as his partner.

The Moffett Building stood at the corner of Griswold and Fort streets, where the Penobscot Building now stands. The rent for the new law office was $20 a month. The space comprised one large office with an inner office partitioned to form two small rooms.

George found four men to rent desk space in the outer office at the rate of $5 each a month. This took care of the office rent, and the young partners' expense was telephone and stationery. Even this was beyond George's ability to pay if he left the Caille Brothers Company, but as usual with money problems, he found the solution—a night bookkeeping job. And he quit his factory job to become a lawyer!

He was cleaning out his desk at the old job, when his

friends gathered round to wish him well. He held up a handful of books.

"Anybody want these?"

"Leave them, George." This was from Howard O. Pierce, with whom he had worked for the past months and who lived within a couple of blocks of his home. Howard put out his hand.

"I'm wishing you all the best, George–but we'll miss you around here."

More prophetic than he knew, George answered, "Maybe we'll be working together on something some day. Who knows?"

"I'd like that." And the men parted.

V

ARTHUR CAILLE, PRESIDENT OF Caille Brothers, whose firm George had just left, and John H. Kunsky, a superintendent in the factory of Caille Brothers, had formed the Casino Company and built three theatres, twenty feet wide and not much longer. They were the Star at 93 Gratiot Avenue, the Royal at 34 Monroe and Farmer streets, and the Casino at 28 Monroe. George worked out an agreement with the men to take care of their bookkeeping at night for $15 a week. Of this sum, George gave his mother $5 and put $10 into the law partnership. The proceeds from this partnership were to be split at the end of each month. George told his mother, "Mother, I have this thing worked out."

But it was 1908, and there was some hesitancy about accepting anything connected with the theatre as legitimate. The mother was something short of enthusiastic.

"I don't know, George—I thought you would be a minister. If you changed your mind about that, all right. But now I think you will be a fine lawyer, and then maybe—no, not maybe—for sure, you will be a judge!"

"Now, Mother"—and his tone was affectionate—"I am only keeping books for the outfit because I need money for expenses. I am not in the entertainment business, but I think I might like to be."

"It's a nickel and dime business—even if you overlook the kind of people in the business. You can't get rich in the entertainment business."

"It won't always be a nickel and dime business."

"These ideas—you got them from those dime novels that you sneaked into the house and read."

"Mo-o-o-ther!"

"I know," said his mother—"I read most of them myself."

"Well?"

"I enjoyed them too, George. That Nick Carter—what a detective! That James Fenimore Cooper—he could write. And those 'Go West' books by Alger. Of course, I enjoyed them."

"Well, Mother—a judge maybe?" and the mother laughed. The conversation ended with a quick hug and a warm togetherness, as it always did with these two.

George was launched on his new career—law—but his living expenses and later on, because of his connection with Caille and Kunsky, most of his clients came from the entertainment field.

The first client was the American Window Cleaning Company, owned by Benjamin Bernstein, whom George described as a "very fine gentleman who was exceedingly sharp in many ways."

The Zanger Fur Company had used the company to do their window cleaning, but when the time came for payment, they refused. Ben asked George to sue.

When the suit came up in court, Ben presented signed slips as receipts which proved the work had been done, and the court gave him a judgment.

"Ben," asked George, when they got outside the courtroom, "why didn't you tell me you had those receipts?"

Ben scratched behind his ear and grinned. "You know that dumb foreman of mine. Sometimes he doesn't get those slips signed. He does the work all right, but he doesn't always get the receipt signed. Now, this work was done. I know it was done, Zanger knows it was done. He admitted it to me, but he laughed and said it was up to me to get receipts. So I just took some old receipts and changed the dates."

"But, Ben, that's terrible. Why did you do this to me?"

"I knew that if I told you, George, you wouldn't go along with that. Anyway, right is right—I was right and we won, didn't we?" In a moment he said, "George, if you are worried that I am not telling the truth, I'll call Zanger; you listen in on the phone. You'll learn that we are right."

"No, Ben, I trust you." It was George's first case for Bernstein. He had another one later.

There was beginning to be some dissatisfaction on George's part with the law partnership. George liked work. Long hours never disturbed him. Difficult situations, in his work, did not discourage him; rather, they served as a challenge. But he would not allow himself to be disadvantaged for someone else–and he expected each person to do his own share. He soon found that his partner, Edmond Stafford, felt that his clientele would be built up by social contacts and spent his time making new ones. The situation was unpalatable to George, and remembering that "he travels the fastest who travels alone," asked Stafford to be released from the partnership. Stafford agreed.

Thereupon George moved across the hall from his old office and manipulated the same deal of renting the outer office space. He kept his affiliation with the motion-picture people. This connection brought in several new clients, and he took on all the law work for them.

He asked for more money for his bookkeeping and got it, as well as all the law work for the Casino Company. The Casino Company now had another theatre, the Empress, and George was delighted with this part of his work. In fact, he gave more attention to the theatre end of his practice than to any other. He could feel the possibility of growth here. This was his new-found love.

He told his mother, "Now they own four theatres, Mother. Four–think of it."

"Yes?" Her tone was neither encouraging nor discouraging. It had a lack of enthusiasm, but she listened to this son of hers.

"Mother, this will be a big, big business one day! You watch and see! More and more people will be theatregoers."

She nodded, her face expressionless.

"But, Mother, don't you see? I know you want me to do some good in this world. And I will! I promise you."

"But right now you want to make money? Is that it?"

His tone was placating. "Well, Mother, that goes with it–but you yourself mentioned that the books, the Alger books, furnished me with ambition."

"Not alone, son. Ambition you were born with." And in a moment, "Now, what happens to your ambition to be a lawyer?"

"That I have–I am a lawyer. But I can reach more people through entertainment, don't you see? Maybe I can give young people what the books gave me–something to aim at, something to look up to."

It was clear that his mother was unconvinced, but here, for George, was an opportunity to grow and possibly to give!

Just then his sister Clara walked through the kitchen, having caught the end of the discussion.

"Hey, George, you still going to be a millionaire?"

Behind her came Minnie. "Leave him alone," Minnie said, "I think he'll make it. Just remember this, George: if you're going to get rich, you've got to be good!"

"Don't worry, Min, I'll be good!"

VI

George entered this new phase of his life with enthusiasm. Motion pictures would, he thought, some day be a very big thing, and he wanted his share of it. At that time theatres were really just converted store buildings, about twenty feet wide, and he felt that a more comfortable space for an audience would contribute to capacity. No one could have foreseen the opulence of the motion-picture theatre of the forties —the Michigan Theatre, the Fisher, the United Artists. It was said that some of the ceilings were decorated with real gold leaf. All George could envision at that time was the need for more space for audiences. And so he went out and located a piece of vacant property which would accommodate theatre needs. It was a five-pointed piece of property—alley property—surrounded by Cadillac Square, Monroe Street and Farmer Street.

The partners Caille and Kunsky went down to look at it but couldn't see the possibility. It was surrounded by alley and lacked an entrance. But they gave George permission to go ahead and try to work out a plan whereby it could be used. Here, then, was George's first bit of financial wizardry, if one could call it that, but certainly it was very resourceful planning. He made a deal with the owner to lease twenty feet of property on Monroe Street. He then went before the Common Council of the City of Detroit for permission to bridge the alley. It was granted.

"Mr. Kunsky," said George, "we have the property and the permission. I have talked to an architect, and we can go ahead whenever you are ready."

"Whenever we can arrange the financial end of it, George, we're ready."

The upshot was the organization of a new company for $125,000. George personally sold $60,000 worth of stock. The other $65,000 was promotion stock. Each partner put up $5,000 and received $30,000 worth of promotion stock for it. George was given $5,000 worth of promotion stock for selling the $60,000 worth of stock for cash. This was enough to build the project.

The Columbia Theatre was an immediate success. The capital stock began paying cash dividends. The building cost was paid in eighteen months. More important to George, he had had this opportunity to show his ability as a financier.

The Columbia Theatre was Kunsky's favorite of all his investments. It was beautiful! When permission had been granted to bridge the alley, permission was also granted to put down canvas at each side of the alley exit after six o'clock so that the alley was blocked off. The entrance was dressed up in a fine manner. Caille and Kunsky were proud. That most of it was George's idea didn't occur to them, or if it did, they never mentioned it.

Arthur Caille was one of the owners of Caille Motors. He and John H. Kunsky were fast friends for many years while Kunsky was employed in the Caille Company and later on, as well. Although Kunsky had little formal education, he had a sharp eye for a business opportunity and while he sat at his bench at Caille Company making parts for the machines which they manufactured, an idea occurred to him.

He bought some slot machines, gum machines and candy machines and set them up in various roadhouses along the shoreline in Canada. Each week he would travel the shoreline, open the machines, make the proper payment to the lessees and repair the machines if necessary. He thus built up a rather sizable capital fund.

Some slot-machine owners had a special "knock-down" gimmick. Every third coin dropped into a soft leather sack that had been inserted in the back of the machine! The owner, when he collected the coins, would pick up one machine, leaving another, and when he got into his car, remove the leather sack, which left him with double the amount stipulated in his agreement with the proprieter of the establishment where the machine was being rented. No one could say that John H. Kunsky resorted to such means. In all matters he was scrupulously honest.

Because of this perhaps, it was to him that Arthur Caille came for financing when he had the idea of opening a penny arcade at the foot of the Belle Isle bridge. Arthur continued at Caille Motors, while Kunsky ran the arcade.

George continued as bookkeeper evenings and as a lawyer by day.

The arrangement remained the same. The five theatres were doing such good business that Arthur wanted to expand again. It was at their regular monthly meeting that he brought the matter up.

"John, that penny arcade is doing well!"

"Yes, Mr. Caille," said George, who now sat in on the business meetings.

"Pretty well," agreed Kunsky.

"Do you think the idea might go pretty well right downtown on Woodward Avenue?"

"No," said Kunsky. "It is a different thing at the bridge approach–people are on their way to have a good time. Right downtown they are on their way to business or shopping."

"John, they would come downtown if we made it attractive."

"That's right–but I don't think it will work. Why don't you forget it, Arthur?"

Had either of them asked George right then, he would have agreed with Kunsky, but neither man was in the habit of consulting him, and Kunsky finally, after a month or two, gave in and allowed the project to go forward. He was not pleased.

Arthur was elated. "We'll call it the Hippodrome. There is a five-story building on Woodward Avenue that we can take over."

"If you mean the Goldberg Building, it's too big."

"Expansion," said Arthur Caille—"you have to have expansion—and that would give us room."

Kunsky was unconvinced, but the project went forward. He acquiesced. It should be called the Hippodrome. And it should contain a variety of entertainment, different on each of the five floors.

The first floor had a little ten-cent show which ran almost continuously. The second floor had glass blowers and other so-called scientific stunts. The third floor had "freaks," humanity in unusual forms, doing the only thing left to them, making a living by capitalizing on their misshapen bodies or other misfortunes. The fourth floor had counters of novelties for sale. This left the fifth floor vacant.

In New York City there was an importer of wild animals with a continuous problem of quarters for them. These animals came into New York from trappers in Africa, sometimes before the importer had orders for them. Until their sale and shipment he had to find quarters for them.

It seemed a good opportunity to George, who straightway went to New York with Caille, and they made an offer to absorb freight charges and house and feed the animals in exchange for a continuing flow of animals, so that the Hippodrome was supplied with new animals as the old ones were shipped out, free of charge except for the small expense of transportation and feed.

A gala opening was planned for this portion of the Hippodrome. The mayor, the city council, other theatre owners and leading lights of some civic organizations were all invited.

Among the last group was a lovely lady who shall remain nameless, for her sake and ours. In the days of laces, ruffles and other furbelows, this lady dressed in the very latest style. Her hair was done atop her head in curls held in place with an invisible net. Dressed as she was with meticulous care, her manner matched.

The animals were caged with a narrow walk between the guard rail and the cages. The animals were duly admired. Since they had recently come from their native habitat, none were trained. They were comparatively calm, as curious about this audience as the audience was about them. That is, until they came to the cage of the black panther.

Everyone stopped. The panther was a deep black, his coat gleamed, and the muscles beneath the coat gave the impression of tremendous power. He commanded respect as he strode up and down in measured steps. The entire group was fascinated. The panther continued his pacing, up and down, until he came directly in front of our "lovely lady."

Suddenly she screamed. Her entire front was soaked from the waist down! She was furious. She looked directly into Kunsky's face and screamed, "Animals!" Kunsky was never quite sure whether she protested the animal's behavior or blamed him for it. The damaged clothing was replaced subsequently, and an apology was sent out and accepted. A plate glass was installed in front of the entire cage about three feet up from the floor, and all seemed well, but Kunsky liked the Hippodrome even less after that affair, and the friendship between Caille and Kunsky suffered during this period.

VII

IN THE YEAR 1912, George and Kathryn Mylne were married.

Just as they were about to leave for the depot and board the train for Washington, Kunsky telephoned, "Stop at our Hippodrome in Toledo, will you, please, George?"

In Toledo George was consulting with the manager of the Hippodrome. Kathryn was standing by, when loud shrieks followed by wails and cries for help were heard.

"What's that?"

"I don't know," said the manager, "but it's coming from the men's room."

George placed his bride in the custody of an attendant and hurried to the men's room. What he saw there would have broken up anyone, but he didn't laugh.

Sitting on the stool and securely wedged in was a little fellow from the third "freak" floor. Short and round with a small shining face, he was known as Billiken. The little face was now distorted with pain and panic. George tugged and the manager tugged, but Billiken was wedged in securely.

"Get me a hammer and a screwdriver," called George, and now Billiken yelled all the louder, this time frightened by his rescuers. The seat was removed, unscrewed from the porcelain bowl, and sawed partially through to release the little man.

"Whew," thought George, "what a way to start a honey-moon!"

Seated in the parlor car, on their way to Washington, the newlyweds talked. George reminisced. He told Kathryn, when she admired his new suit, about the clothing that his mother used to make for him and the girls; about the yearly suit of clothes he was given each Christmas—"my first store-bought clothes!"

He looked out the window; neither spoke for a while. Then, encouraged by the sense of privacy the click of the rails and the noise of the engine provided, the man went on, "I remember my first derby hat. I bought it when I first returned from St. Louis. You have no idea what a derby hat does for a man. I put it on and immediately I felt 'jaunty.' Bob Billings, who lived next door to us, asked me to go roller skating. I had never skated before, but I was sure that anything Bob could do, I could do. We went down to the Light Guard Armory on Congress Street. It had been fitted up into a roller rink. Across the center of the floor they had put a hump–whether to improve drainage or test the skill of the skater, I don't know. I skated around the rink one time, holding onto the wall as I went. I was satisfied that I was a natural at this sport, so I started out. When I came to the rise in the floor, I went up with the rise, my feet flew out from under me, my hat came off. I went up in the air and came down–you guessed it–right on my derby hat. I never roller-skated again."

Kathryn laughed and laughed, and George, a little ruefully, joined in. The next day the laugh was on Kathryn.

Dresses were more complicated in 1912–tiny waistlines, long skirts to be held gracefully to one side, sleeves puffed at the shoulders and long and lacy at the cuffs. But the *pièce de résistance* was the hat.

The hats were large with just the proper dip of the brim into which the tip of an ostrich plume nestled, hemmed in by other plumes on either side. Kathryn's hat was a thing of beauty.

The weather in Washington was wonderful, the day bright and balmy, and George was showing Kathryn the city. She carried her parasol unopened as they walked around the park. She noticed that other women had their parasols opened and held high overhead, but she was loath to cover the large and beautiful hat.

"The women are admiring your elegant hat," said George.

Kathryn nodded, pleased. "It is warm, though," she said, taking it off. There was a sudden flurry, and two little birds flew out. In dismay Kathryn realized what the women had been staring at, for the little birds had stripped pieces off the feathers and the hat was all but ruined.

George comforted her. Said he, "Those birds will have the prettiest nests in this city."

Their own nest back in Detroit was a newly built house on Pallister Avenue. All his life George had dreamed of a bathroom with a shower large enough so that he could stand in the middle, stretch his arms out and still be clear of the walls. Such a bathroom was in the new house. The rest of the planning he left to the architect and his wife, but the bathroom was his own idea. Later he wondered if he had been wise. His tendency to frequent showers contributed, he thought, to his early baldness. It was a blow to his pride to lose his hair, but he didn't submit easily. He took the "Thomas" treatments. He bought gadgets and ointments. But it was all to no avail—the hair was gone.

VIII

THE THEATRES WERE GOING WELL, but not the partners Kunsky and Caille. The Hippodrome was a losing cause, but the partnership might have survived even that except that both men tired. Each of them confided in George, separately.

"George," said Kunsky, "I am sick and tired of that Hippodrome, and I am sick and tired of arguing with Arthur."

"Why don't you buy him out?"

Kunsky shook his head. "I just don't have the money to buy him out."

George nodded in sympathy. "Could Mr. Caille be persuaded to buy you out?"

Kunsky again shook his head. "He doesn't have the money either." Kunsky saw a gleam of light. "I'll tell you what, George. If you can think up some scheme to get rid of Arthur, to raise the money, I can raise your salary."

George looked up. "How much?"

"Well, you would get three thousand a year. I'll move my offices into the Dime Bank Building. You already have your law offices there."

George had not quite figured out a way or even made up his mind to get into the disagreement between the partners, when he met Caille in the hall.

"How are things?" he asked.

Caille responded, "Not so good, George. I hate to admit it to Kunsky, but I'd certainly like to find a way out of this whole deal."

"Do you mean the partnership?"

Caille flared. "Yes, I do, and if you can think of any way for me to get rid of my stock for what it is worth—that is, forty-five thousand dollars, or thirty thousand in cash and fifteen thousand in notes–I'll pay you five per cent on the cash payment."

"Fifteen hundred dollars?"

"That's right."

"Do you know of any prospective buyer? Maybe Mr. Kunsky?"

"I don't want Kunsky to have it, but we don't have to worry, because Kunsky doesn't have the money. No, there are no restrictions as to the buyer."

"I'll sure think about it, Mr. Caille."

It was early the next day that he approached Kunsky. "If I can find a buyer for your stock, will you sell, Mr. Kunsky?"

Kunsky looked at George, then looked away. He didn't want to sell out.

"Mr. Kunsky," began George, "I can get a buyer for the thirty thousand dollars."

"Who?"

"Mr. Frank Westbrook. Remember him?"

"Does he want the stock?"

"Well, he will buy it. Then we can offer Arthur Caille forty-five thousand dollars for his stock, fifteen thousand of which will be paid in notes. That way you will have the same amount of stock that you have now and all you will be paying is the fifteen thousand dollars in notes for his entire holdings."

The deal went through exactly as George planned it. His salary went up to $3,000 a year, and the theatre offices were moved to the Dime Bank Building. He now had a law practice as well as the salary. An added advantage of those times was that no income tax was paid on less than $3,000. A married man with an income of $10,000 paid about $60 in tax.

But the deal brought some displeasure, and Caille's indignation was difficult for George. Still, as Caille seemed to forget, the deal was the result of his own discontent with Kunsky and the partnership. As Caille flared out at George he was reminded of that by George and of the fact that he had offered $1,500 to George to sell his stock. Caille, in his anger, said, "I am very disappointed that you would treat me like this, George, but a deal is a deal, and you'll get your money as soon as I get mine from Mr. Kunsky."

George drew up a contract dissolving the partnership. The two men studied their copies and met to finalize it. Then Caille, reading aloud, came to the clause which stipulated that he could not go into the theatre business in Detroit for five years.

"John, for God's sake, do you think I would do a thing like that to you?"

Kunsky looked noncommittal.

Caille continued, "So you have no faith whatever in me—after all we have been through together. You should know that I wouldn't compete with you. You—"

George broke in, but Caille said, "Never mind, George, I know you must protect John's interest. But, John, why would you leave this in a contract between old friends?"

Kunsky looked at George. "Take it out, George."

George remonstrated, "But, Mr. Kunsky, it is standard practice in cases like this."

"That's right, George—any good lawyer would feel as you do. But just take it out."

"Mr. Kunsky, if he goes back into the business, don't blame me."

And the clause was taken out.

Three months later Arthur Caille promoted the Majestic Theatre on Woodward Avenue, near Harper Hospital.

The deal had been closed except for the part between Arthur Caille and George—that is, the $1,500 that he had been promised. George reminded him of that.

"That's right. A deal is a deal, and I made one with you, George."

"You said you were about to turn your car in for sixteen hundred dollars. Why don't you give me the car instead of money?"

"Fine, if you'll pay one hundred dollars. That's the difference."

George paid him and was the owner of a Cadillac coupe, his first car. Black-walnut ceiling, silver vase, carved fittings—it was the last word in grandeur. And George, who had never driven a car in his life, asked the salesman at Cadillac, "Drive me around the block a couple of times; I want to get accustomed to this car." After that, with no more instruction than the position of the various parts, he got into the driver's seat and drove home. He parked in front of his house on Pallister Avenue, called his wife to show the new possession to her, then drove to the back of the house, where the garage opened onto the alley.

A one-car garage and a narrow alley—it was quite a job, back and forth, back and forth, until he had the car in direct line with the garage door. He was about to put his foot on the brake, get out and open the doors, but unaccustomed to driving, he put his foot on the accelerator instead, and the car shot right through the door! There was little damage to the car, but the garage doors had to be replaced.

"Still," said George as he recounted his experience, "I had a Cadillac car."

His next trip was down to show his mother. She was delighted.

Clients were frequent now. George had many of the theatre accounts, and once they retained him, they rarely left for another attorney.

About this time his first client, Ben Bernstein of the American Window Cleaning Company, came back to him. This time he needed defending in a lawsuit.

Ben's company had been cleaning windows at the Newton Annis Company, a building now occupied by Richmond Brothers, a men's clothing store. The windows on the second floor were what is called in the trade "vertical pivoted"–that is, they turned from left to right on a pivot in the center of the window. One of the workmen leaned a ladder against the window. It broke, and the glass fell to Woodward Avenue below. A female passerby was cut on the ankle.

She promptly engaged Sherman Callender, one of Detroit's better-known attorneys. Sherman sued all three: the tenant, Newton Annis; the owners of the building; and the American Window Cleaning Company. Moynihan and Moynihan represented the Newton Annis Company; Oxtoby and Oxtoby represented the building's owners; and George W. Trendle represented the American Window Cleaning Company, or Ben Bernstein.

When the case came up, George thought the best defense for his client would be to spread the blame. Obviously the woman was entitled to damages, but just as obviously she asked far too much.

Having questioned and coached Ben carefully, George went into court on the theory that Bernstein took his orders from Newton Annis Company as to where he would work and in what sequence and was therefore not a contractor but an employee of Newton Annis'. This threw the case into a labor question and would imply that the other two defendants were at fault.

A quick session was called by the other two defendants. They urged George to stop that line of defense and offered to share in the settlement. George agreed on condition that he could not control his client when he got to the stand. Ben proved a very good witness for himself!

Back into conference the attorneys went. The plaintiff's attorney saw his case weakening and offered to settle for

$3,000, each of the three defendants paying $1,000. The offer was accepted.

Bernstein went over to the office of the plaintiff's attorney, Sherman Callender, and gave him a "poor mouth"—a pitiful story of his own impoverished state. Sherman accepted $200 in cash, with notes for the other $800. Later, when the $800 was not paid, Sherman, convinced that suing Ben would be a lost cause, settled for $600 in cash.

But this case so impressed Sherman Callender that he asked George if he would combine in a partnership with him and Walter Trevor, the assistant prosecutor. George accepted and moved into the Dime Bank Building.

Bernstein moved to Philadelphia. Coming to Detroit years later, he arrived at George's office and sent word in to him that an old friend wished to see him. George had changed so much that Ben didn't recognize him. He had put on considerable weight, and lost much of his hair. He couldn't make Ben believe that he was the same man. Ben left unconvinced, and George never saw him again.

IX

"MOTHER," CALLED GEORGE, as he entered the family home on Brady Street in which she now lived, "would you like to take a ride with me?"

"Of course. I'll get my hat and gloves. Minnie, you find my purse."

It happened often. George would stop in on his way to the office or on his way to the shops or doing errands and take his mother with him. It seemed she was always ready to go! And the car delighted her.

The car delighted her so much that George wished he could take her more often, but he had another idea. When they returned home, he spoke to his father.

"Dad, if I buy a car for you and the girls, will you teach them and Mother how to drive? And allow them to take it out when they want to go for a drive?"

"*Naturlich* [naturally]." His father lapsed into German when he was excited. His eagerness fooled George.

In the parents' home things had gone from bad to worse. The estrangement between his father and the rest of the family deepened. His father shared with many of his generation the patriarchal complex in which the father is the absolute ruler of the family—a concept totally unacceptable to the family. He believed the family's duty lay in supporting him in his ideas, and physically as well.

When Jennie, Minnie and Clara began to work, the elder Trendle stopped contributing to the household upkeep. He maintained the home by paying taxes and making repairs and additions, but the girls paid for groceries, clothing and all incidental expenses for them and their mother. And George from his first job on contributed, even when he was working his way through high school and college. It was natural for him to keep an eye on his mother and sisters.

Now George bought a Paige-Detroit car, used but in excellent condition. It was a middle-class car, not a Cadillac, but not a small car either. His mother and the girls looked forward to the driving lessons.

It was soon obvious that Dad Trendle had no idea of allowing anyone but himself to use the car. The "trips," as he called them, were always dictated by him. He would drive to Wyandotte, turn the car around and come back. George was called in for a conference.

His father made it clear that he believed that women should not be driving cars. "I will take them for rides but they have to go where I want to go, not just silly visiting around."

Angry and frustrated, George decided to take the car back. When he arrived to take it, he found the garage doors chained shut. The wheels of the car had been chained also.

"Where is he?" shouted George.

Mother said, "Let be, George; give him time. Leave the car where it is and I will tell you when the time is right to get it."

Months later she telephoned one morning and said, "Take the car away, George." His father wanted the garage space for other things, she told him, and George drove over to get the car. He was amazed at its condition. The tires had been changed to old worn-out ones; all gasoline had been removed from the tank. George replaced the gasoline and hoped the tires would make it to the Paige-Detroit garage, about two blocks away. In less than a block, smoke began to pour from the engine, and George discovered that the oil had been taken from the engine and the water removed as well.

The Paige-Detroit Company bought the car for $600,

which George turned over to his mother. But the father-son relationship had been worsened. There was no common ground on which the two could meet, and there began a series of harassments, sometimes aimed at the entire family but more often aimed at George.

Often the father would speak of his old home in Germany, his friends and relatives over there, and would voice his desire to be with them. Finally, after consulting the family, George offered to pay his expenses, continue an allowance and let him return to Germany, to Waldshut, where he had been born.

"What about my house?" asked the father.

"You may have the house. I want Mother and the girls in an apartment closer to me."

The house was sold for $4,000. The father left for Germany with that as a nest egg and with a guaranteed remittance from his son. He lived there for years and died there.

His family learned after his death that he had spent his time with his old friends, recounting the days of his youth and dwelling particularly on the "good old days in Norwalk," where he had been a leader in the politics of the city and a person of influence.

Lost opportunities built themselves up in his memory. He told of the father and uncle of the Fisher brothers, who had a blacksmith shop in Norwalk, where they made forgings. The two Fishers owned the business, and Dad Trendle was the third man in the shop, never an owner. The Fishers left Norwalk to go to Detroit in the carriage business, and Dad Trendle went into his own business. The Fisher sons had other ideas. They left the original company to try their hand in the new automobile industry. A man named Mendlesohn put up the money for a plant, and the Fishers were employed at what was later the General Motors Corporation.

"I might have gone with them," Dad Trendle would say,

"but I didn't." He bragged of his family in America and especially of his son's success.

He became interested in the civic affairs of the little town and grew to be rather well known. When he died, he left a will, bequeathing his entire estate–a matter of $900–to his son. George turned it over to his mother.

X

It was 1915. George Trendle was attorney and general manager of the theatres of the John H. Kunsky Enterprises. His offices were on the seventeenth floor of the Dime Bank Building. The theatre offices were on the twentieth. Often he would leave his office and walk across Woodward Avenue and the Campus Martius to visit the theatres, one by one.

This day, as he walked along, he noted mentally that the neighborhood was not what it had been. In fact, there had been an influx of cheap little businesses. "This area is going downhill," he thought. He was glad to reach Monroe Street, where his friend Howard O. Pierce managed the Liberty Theatre. The old Scotch Presbyterian Church had been sold and was now, after many alterations, a theatre. The architect had placed on the outside wall, facing Farmer Street, five panels about twelve feet high and six feet wide.

"Howard," asked George, "don't you think we might lend an air of culture to this place if we had some quotations from Shakespeare painted on these panels?"

"I'm not a student of Shakespeare."

"You're an ex-actor, Howard; I'm sure you can find a few random quotations to put there. Anyway, the public library is right across the street."

Howard spent the next two mornings at the public library and came up with little or nothing. "All the world's a stage" was the extent of his study. He telephoned George that his search was fruitless.

"You'll come up with something. Just keep at it." Howard wrote the other four mottoes himself, had them painted on the panels and called George to see them.

"I knew you'd make it," said George.

Howard expostulated, "Come on, George, you know I wrote these things myself."

George laughed. "Well, as long as I don't know who wrote them."

"I'm glad to be rid of that assignment. Now I can get back to other work." Later on, as Howard stood in one corner of the theatre he could hear some of the patrons discussing the mottoes. All agreed that they were very fitting. The daily press mentioned the quotations favorably, and George and Howard were very amused.

Howard had a particular aptitude for this kind of work. George asked him to come into the main office and handle the publicity for all the theatres. He accepted.

Howard had been, for a short time, a vaudeville actor, and he understood these people. Further, he was a gifted cartoonist and could work up his own illustrations for the newspaper advertisements. The *Weekly Film News* was written by Howard. The greats of the day appeared in his paper. On February 7, 1915, the frontispiece was a picture of Rhea Haines. Inside, over the caption "A true queen of beauty," was a picture of Lillian Russell. The Washington Theatre had Gaby Deslys, and the Famous Pictures Film Production starred Mary Pickford. The same week the Liberty Theatre held over Hobert Boswell in *Buckshot John*. Lillian Russell starred in *Wildfire* at the Alhambra.

Vaudeville acts were booked and shown, but George felt they could do very well by producing their own shows. When he talked it over with Howard, he met with enthusiasm. He planned to go ahead with Howard as producer. He strode across the park toward his office, but he couldn't get rid of the idea that Monroe Street was overrun with honky-tonk businesses and that the center of the theatre world in Detroit should be moved farther north.

Instead of stopping in his own offices, he went straight to the twentieth floor to Kunsky's office.

"Well, George?"

"I just came from the Liberty, and while it looks pretty good, have you noticed how dilapidated some of the buildings are in that area?"

Kunsky, sensing the approach of a proposition, was cagey. "Oh, I don't know, George. What's on your mind?"

"I think the time is right for a change. The center of the theatre district should move father uptown with the better business houses."

"Think it over, George."

And George, thinking it over, found a piece of property facing Grand Circus Park. He took his information to Kunsky.

"A theatre facing the park, Mr. Kunsky, would be a very good investment, I think."

But Kunsky was not sold so easily. "All I have to put into it, George, is twenty-five thousand dollars. If you think you can promote a new theatre building on that, I'll go along."

That was all the encouragement George needed. He went straightway to the owner of this property on Broadway and another facing the park and arranged a ninety-nine-year lease on both pieces of property with the provision that a project containing both theatre and a five-story office building at a cost of not less than $300,000 be built. Then he went to work—first, with Kunsky, who said, "George, if you can put this one over you will get a twenty-five per cent interest in the promotion." George agreed.

He arranged to get a loan of $200,000 from Tillotson and Wolcott Company in Cleveland. The Sissman Contracting Company in Detroit agreed to take $75,000 of their contract in deferred payments, and their subcontractors agreed to do the same.

When the theatre building was finished, it cost $350,000, and all the Kunsky firm had in it was $25,000. All of the rest had been arranged by George. But it was not, by any means, all beer and skittles while the financing was going on. Kunsky grew apprehensive and complained that he was afraid that he would lose his $25,000. He refused to talk financing with anyone. George was young and looked even younger, he was not seasoned in financial circles, and the principals wanted to talk with Mr. Kunsky. But Kunsky, fearing further involvement, refused to meet any of them.

"I think you're getting sour on the whole affair," George told him angrily.

"It's possible," returned Kunsky, equally exasperated.

George strode out of the office.

A good brisk walk was his usual antidote for anger, and he started up Woodward Avenue, when he was greeted by an old friend. It was Mark Freud. "What's wrong, George?"

And George, glad to get it off his chest, told him the story. Freud became quite interested in the plan and told George, "Go back up there, offer to return his twenty-five thousand dollars, and tell him you can get the money elsewhere. I'll put up the money, and I'll give you a fifty per cent interest."

George went back to the office. "Mr. Kunsky, if you are still worried about your money, I can get it back for you."

"What do you mean by that?"

George told him of Freud's offer and this brought, "Now, that's a hell of a note, George. You went into this thing with me. You should stay with me."

"I'd like to, Mr. Kunsky, but–"

Kunsky interrupted, "Are you trying to sell me out now that you have a new backer and a higher percentage?"

"That's not it–I made an agreement with you and I am glad to stay with it. But I cannot do a proper job with your complaining. I have got to have a free hand and I have got to know that you are behind me."

From then on George was given an absolutely free hand, and on February 1, 1918, the Madison Theatre was opened. There was a long lineup of patrons on opening night. The Madison was an instantaneous success!

On February 22, 1918, George's first-born, a son, arrived. There had been the usual discussion of names, and the family again had settled on "William" in deference to George's mother's wishes. His wife concurred, but the boy was born on Washington's birthday, and the family felt the coincidence could not be ignored, so he also was named George Washington Trendle.

George had little time to celebrate, however. His friend Howard O. Pierce had gone into the Army. This was World War I. Howard was single and free, and he knew that he had a special talent which could be useful, so he enlisted in Special Services and was put in charge of the forty-two Liberty theatres located in army camps all over the United States. He was commissioned a major.

George had ached to go along. When Howard telephoned, as he often did, George told him that now he could get his affairs in order and leave. So far his draft status had been "deferred" because he had two children. He felt that he could enlist and be accepted.

It had been established that he would be commissioned major just as Howard had been, and that his field would be the European theatre, operating for our troops over there. The acts would be engaged over here and sent to Europe.

It was late October, and George, satisfied that neither his business nor his family would suffer from his absence, sat back to await his call to the Army. He was eager to go.

On November 11, 1918, the war was over! Bells rang, whistles were blown, a hastily organized dance band played on Washington Boulevard, and dancing in the street was happy and gay. The corner of Woodward Avenue and Madison was a solid mass of people milling around. All restraint was thrown off–strangers kissed and hugged and danced!

George never had his opportunity to serve his country in the Army.

XI

Early in 1918 his mother telephoned. Immediately she said, "I'm worried about Min, George. This doctor isn't helping her."

Minnie had developed tuberculosis and had been taking medication and living out of doors—on a sleeping porch—for a month.

"Mother, would you consider sending Min to Arizona?"

"If it will help her, anywhere, George."

In the days before wonder drugs, tuberculosis was almost always fatal, but sometimes, in clear high air with little humidity, it could be arrested. Min went to Arizona.

In about a year she became restless and urged her doctor to send her back to Michigan. She was better—he pronounced her case "arrested"—and she started home. But she stopped in Colorado for some sightseeing, caught cold and arrived in Detroit a very sick person.

A sleeping porch was fixed up in George's own home and Minnie was brought there, but nothing helped, and in 1919 Minnie died.

Business was doing extraordinarily well, at the newly opened Madison Theatre in particular. At the end of the first year the partners counted their profit. The Madison alone had netted them $400,000.

"What do you say, George? Shall we take the money out of the business and divide? Twenty-five per cent is yours."

George was more than willing. And so $100,000 went to George and $300,000 to Kunsky. Kunsky looked at the check and said, "I never believed it could happen. Oh, a little profit maybe, or even a lot, but this is more than I had ever hoped for."

"Well, I was sure it could happen, and I have been planning what to do with it. I want to build a new house."

"I think I will build one too," said Kunsky.

George built his house on LaSalle Boulevard. The plans called for an expenditure of about $27,000, but when it was finished and furnished, more than $80,000 had been spent.

Kunsky's experience paralleled George's. His house, planned for $75,000, actually cost $250,000. Still, both men were proud and happy.

It was sometime near the close of World War I that Kunsky made a remark that George never forgot. They had been going over their receipts. The war had cut deeply into their profit. There were fuelless nights, lightless nights, a shortage of experienced help; and one night the partners sat in their offices taking stock. A stack of unpaid bills lay before them. Suddenly Kunsky said, "George, even if the whole thing goes to hell, we'll still have a couple of nice houses with no mortgages." He smiled for a moment. "We'll come out all right."

They had come a long way from the days of store buildings with collapsible chairs. Kunsky would think back and occasionally mention the old days. Projection was once a hand-wound operation. A huge basket was set at the foot of the machine to catch the film. At the end of the picture the operator had to be very quick to catch the end of the film so that he could begin to rewind without having to untangle the whole mess. Film breaks were frequent, and they always seemed to happen at the most crucial point of the picture. A slide flashed on the screen, "Just a moment, please," was the signal for clapping, stamping of feet–in short, bedlam, a break for the audience, a chance to release emotion. Great fun!

Just before the start of the main feature another slide flashed, "Ladies, please remove your hats"–with good reason, for most women wore very large hats.

In the pit the pianist improvised music to fit the action on the screen. The audience shed tears to the tunes of "Hearts and Flowers," "Memories" and sometimes the "Rosary"! Indians rode over the hill to the tune of "Nola." Some pictures still considered great were shown: for example, *Mender of the Nets* with Mabel Normand and in 1914 *The Birth of a Nation.*

And John H. Kunsky, who had long played with the idea of Americanizing his name, took legal steps to do so. His name was changed to John H. King, and from this page on he will be referred to by his new name.

If John H. King spent time reminiscing, his partner had little time to do so. His own son, George junior, nicknamed Bud, was growing into a fine healthy boy. On October 24, 1919, he was joined by his sister, Mary Kathryn, who was immediately called Mary K. Their father, never needing an excuse for hard work, for he loved it, now had added impetus in his drive for success. As usual he was on the lookout for new business ventures.

Walking in the business district downtown one day, he remembered that the street corners from the building line to the curb belonged to the city. That is, the corners themselves belonged to the city. And George had his idea!

He found a client who might be willing to pay for the paving of all these corners for the city if he were allowed to place some advertising in the pavement. Subsequently sketches of the advertising were drawn up to be presented to the city council. Then he engaged an attorney with considerable political influence to represent him in the deal. The attorney was John McKay. The city was to get a percentage of the advertising money, and the proposition looked certain to be passed by the city council, when a totally unforeseen thing happened.

Two days before the idea was to be presented, a newspaper carried the headline "Council Men Questioned on Bribery."

There was a great hullabaloo, and two councilmen were questioned closely. During the questioning all business, including the paving idea, was discussed or at least mentioned.

John McKay telephoned George, "I don't want to go ahead with this under the circumstances."

"But, John, no bribe has been offered, and I don't intend to pay any. This is a legitimate advertising scheme."

"I want to get out of it," said John.

That afternoon George received a telephone call from the prosecuting attorney, who was also an old fraternity brother of George's.

"Let it go for the present, George," said the attorney. "The newspapers are going to have a picnic with this affair and you would come in for some bad publicity."

"I am clean–I've done nothing wrong. This is a legitimate offer, and I'm sure the city can make some money from it."

"You know how it is, George. Your reputation would take a beating no matter which way this questioning turned."

George gave up the idea, thinking to go back to it later, but he never did. At the time a couple of council members were judged guilty and went to jail; the city lost faith in many of their elected officials.

Not long afterward George said, "Mr. King, we still can get the leases on that Broadway property"; then, laughing, "do you think you have recovered enough from the Madison Theatre to sail into another deal?"

King smiled. After the opening of the Madison Theatre, the theatre offices and George's offices had been moved to the Madison Building. King's office faced Grand Circus Park.

Now King looked out the window, down at the park. The seats that lined the walks were occupied by young and old. The old read or fed pigeons; the young engaged in horseplay, knocking one another off the ends of the seats. Some climbed up and over the statue of Hazen S. Pingree. In the center was the new fountain, pretty by day but beautiful by night, when the colored lights played over it. No doubt about it–John H. King loved this city. He turned back to his partner.

"What kind of deal, George?"

While George explained that a second theatre in the same area would draw more people to the area and be different enough to make its own audience, King remembered.

He had felt from the first time he met George that George would bring him luck. He saw the young man, seated on a high stool at the Caille Motor Company, apart from the rest of the office and yet near enough to have full cognizance of all the happenings in the office. He saw one ambitious young man, using his spare time to study from the books which he usually carried under his arm! King had the uneducated man's awe of "book learning." He knew that George would bring him luck. If under "luck" he grouped promotion ideas, financial ideas and ideas for expansion, he was not disappointed. George gave all of them to him. He thought of the days they had been through during the war. Many partnerships did not survive; theirs–his and George's–survived.

There had been the flu epidemic, laying low almost a quarter of the population, during which health officers closed nine out of ten theatres throughout the country. There was the patriotic drive to raise money. Liberty Bonds were sold, and young people were encouraged to give up entertainment and save their pennies for war stamps. Theatres were lucky to break even, but between them he and George were making good headway in all of their theatres.

"Go ahead, George–you go ahead," he reiterated, nodding.

The building was to cost $1,250,000. It would be called the Broadway-Capitol Building and would house the new

Broadway-Capitol Theatre. The capitalization was to be a loan of $500,000 against the Madison Theatre or a joint loan of $1,000,000 against both theatres. The president of the Central Savings Bank, a Mr. Holiday, had investigated thoroughly and had agreed to pay out certain moneys as the building progressed.

Twelve persons were involved in the ownership of the eight pieces of property which would be the building site. George prepared the leases and engaged a real-estate agent, Clark Wormer, Jr., who was a personal friend, to make the arrangements. All twelve owners agreed on the terms of the lease.

A couple of days before the closing of the deal was to take place, George, usually very healthy, was stricken with such pain that he had to be rushed to Providence Hospital at six in the morning. It was discovered by Dr. Panzner, who performed the operation, that his condition was a ruptured appendix. Without sulfanilamide or any of the other miracle drugs, the case looked bad, and Dr. Panzner told King that there was no chance that George would recover and that he had only one course of action left to him–a general washout and drainage. Thanks to the excellent physical condition in which George had kept himself, he did survive and was on his way to complete recovery in a couple of weeks.

On the fourth day after the operation Clark Wormer came to see George. After the usual small talk Clark said, "George, it begins to look as if some of the owners could back out if the lease is not signed at once."

King stood at George's bedside with Wormer.

"Bring in the leases, Mr. King, and the other papers in the file," said George. "I want to look them over."

"Now, George, I'm sure it is all right. We can work this out later on," said King, remembering the doctor's prognosis.

But in a couple of days all the parties met in George's hospital room and signed the papers, and the deal was on.

Two weeks later, recuperating at White Sulphur Springs, George walked with the gallery around the eighteen-hole golf course, with the professional golfers in their tournament. That night the pain was a terrible thing, and George was very sick again.

Recovered, he went to see his doctor, but it was not for years that he was told that what had probably happened was that he had broken the adhesions which were forming and that it was good for his condition. Later, much later, the theory was verified. Now patients are put on their feet sometimes hours after an operation.

XII

New buildings are intriguing things. Joining the usual sidewalk superintendents, George and his partner watched the Broadway-Capitol Building rise from the ground. As arranged, the first payment from the bank was to be paid when the plastering was started. It was to be $50,000.

However, in the meantime, the Central Bank had been sold to the First National Bank, and the president, Mr. Holiday, had been replaced by E. D. Stair, an old acquaintance of George's. For Stair had been the head of Stair and Havlin Vaudeville Circuit. Since the new motion-picture houses had put the vaudeville houses out of business, Stair regarded George and John H. King with some ill feeling.

He refused to confirm the $50,000 loan.

It was a bad setback for George, but he had one out. The contractors were some sixty days behind in their work. A conference was called, and the contractors were told that the delay would result in lawsuits and other trouble over film contracts and that definitely no money would be paid them until they had brought the work up to date. They were given the deadline of New Year's Day. Motion-picture commitments had been made for that day, and the building had to be finished for the opening!

Work began to progress in two or three shifts a day. But the finishing work was incomplete as the opening day drew near. A make-do effort brought out as many American flags as they could find. Red, white and blue bunting covered handrails of raw wood. The unplastered boxes were draped with bunting. The opening was on time and such an immediate success that the Union Mortgage Company offered to refinance the whole deal. And the Capitol Building Corporation (King-

Trendle) put out a bond issue of $1,000,000. Who bought these bonds and kept them until maturity? Well-founded rumors said E. D. Stair!

"Mr. King," said George, "I am sick of the whole banking setup here."

As usual, King nodded, without saying a word.

"You can get a deal all set up, but along comes the new personnel and what happens? The whole arrangement goes out the window, and the money is withdrawn."

"A fellow ought to have his own bank," said King, half joking.

"Why not?" said his partner.

King laughed, but George remained serious.

He located twelve men who shared the same thought and who put up $100,000 each. With $1,400,000, the Griswold State Bank came into being. It was later renamed the Griswold National Bank, and then consolidated with the German-American Bank, whose name it took. The original investors kept their stock and joined with George in the consolidation with the Union Guardian Bank.

About this time Howard O. Pierce was released from his army post and came back to work with George. Both were very pleased with that arrangement.

George Trendle had an almost uncanny ability for picking the right man for a particular job. Once when someone questioned him on this, he said, "I don't know" and thought for a moment.

"What is your secret? You rarely make a mistake," an old friend remarked.

"I guess it is giving a man room to expand. That is, giving a man a chance to do a job his way—and it's a chance to grow! If you hover over an employe, giving directions, you rob him of incentive. You wall him in. Move away, letting him know you have faith in his ability. It is a system which works every time."

George had heard with regularity from Howard during the war years and was anxious to have him back. Most of the motion-picture houses had vaudeville acts between the shows. Balaban and Katz of Chicago were furnishing many of them, but the best of them, said George, were produced in their own theatres by Howard O. Pierce.

All the big names were employed in the theatres of the King-Trendle Enterprises at one time or another. There were Al Jolson, Fannie Brice, Eddie Cantor, Bob Hope, Will Rogers and many, many others. Bob Hope's salary, the books say, was $225 a week.

There was Will Rogers, who had no written material at all. Audiences loved Rogers, who confided in the audience, "All I know is what I read in the papers," simply twirled his rope and posed as not an authority on anything. He was a fine, conscientious performer. Once, when the house was a mediocre one because of a picture which proved unpopular, he offered to play at one of the other King-Trendle theatres without salary to make up for the lack of the audience where he was playing.

Pierce reminisced about the talent. "My job," he said, "was to supply the live talent for the shows. Sometimes, it wasn't very live. Often, when a picture was released, the star would be sent along to help in the promotion by appearing in person."

Such an appearance was made by Nita Naldi, one of the most popular vamp types. Her pictures were always good box office, and Howard looked forward to meeting her. She could with great impact portray human emotion, but in the days of the silent movie she was not called upon to memorize script. She couldn't memorize, she couldn't dance, she couldn't sing. Moreover, she hated public appearances. She told Howard so.

But he still tried to work out a presentable act for her. He wrote a short speech. "I won't learn it," she said.

"You won't have to–I'll stand in the wings and lead you all the way!" Grudgingly she agreed. It was an experience that Howard never forgot.

She was lovely to look at. Her near-perfect figure was gowned in red satin with sequins, beading and a long train. She swept toward the stage to the accompaniment of a pronounced ripping sound. In his eagerness to get as close as possible to Nita during the act, Howard had stepped on her train. She blazed at Howard with a string of profanity that might have startled the well-known mule skinner. She looked down, saw the damage was not going to show, stepped into the footlights and in the sweetest tones, with a smile for her audience, began, "Ladies and gentlemen."

George Trendle often said, "There is no producer of this type of show who can even come close to Howard. Howard had the best of all the shows. Two out of four of the shows in our theatres were produced by Howard, and these were the best of them all."

With a chuckle George remembered Howard's presentation when they were showing the motion picture *Ben Hur*. Howard had a treadmill set up in front of the screen with appropriate scenery behind the treadmill. At appropriate times in the picture the scenery would move, and live horses would gallop on the treadmill. The horses seemed to go round and round. "Live Horses on the Stage" read the advertisements–and they really were!

"Howard discovered many orchestras which later became very famous. There was a former coal miner in Pittsburgh, playing in small local theatres and clubs. Howard brought him to the Broadway-Capitol after a tryout in the State. This man was Russ Morgan, a brilliant musician. It was said of him that his arrangements could be completed by him in one tenth of the time it would take other musicians. He couldn't do all of them, of course, but he had a young musician in his band who was quite gifted. He did many of the arrangements. This was Clyde Trask, who for many years later on furnished the music on the old *River Queen*."

The Michigan Theatre was known to be the most opulent in the country. It seated 4,000, and both King and Trendle considered it the top theatre in their line. Edward Werner led his top orchestra in this top theatre. His men wore maroon uniforms with gold braid and gold buttons. They were elegant. Of all these fancy dressers, John Crisman was the most fastidious. And John had no liking for animals, particularly on the stage.

Howard Pierce had booked Proske's Animal Act. He built a platform and had the performance between the audience and the stage, right next to the orchestra. Every time an animal passed near John Crisman he drew back a little–not enough for the audience, engrossed in the animal act, to notice but furnishing some amusement to the orchestra. Then it happened!

The tiger stepped out of line; drawn by the brilliance of the gold braid and shiny buttons, he stopped in front of John Crisman and just looked! The wildest of all Mack Sennett scenes couldn't exaggerate the next scene. John pushed his chair back into the rest of the orchestra; chairs and musicians flew in all directions. The audience was delighted. The applause was gratifying to Howard, and he would have liked to keep that as part of the act, but not Crisman–and who could depend on the tiger's reacting in the same way next time?

"Howard," said George, "we have every kind of an orchestra, but in this whole city we have no symphony."

"Do you think we need a symphony? How would you tie that in with the movies?"

"You're right; it wouldn't do as an act between the shows. It would have to be a separate thing. But I am convinced that Detroit needs some fine music. And I think it is up to us to do it! We have the facilities!"

Howard called in Edward Werner, leader of the Michigan Theatre orchestra, and asked him if he could form such an orchestra, by taking men from the orchestras in the various theatres. He could and he would, he said. So, from a culling of musicians from the Michigan, Broadway-Capitol and Madison theatres, the first symphony orchestra in the theatre was born.

Werner led the orchestra, and they played at the Broadway-Capitol each Sunday at noon, right after church services. The admission was fifty cents, and the audience could stay with no extra charge for the movie. It was a very popular concert.

Father Coughlin, widely heard "radio priest," wrote to George, "This is a very worthwhile contribution to the culture of Detroit."

XIII

GEORGE LOOKED DOWN at the paper on his desk.

"What the hell is this?" he bellowed. "Get me the bills from the Detroit *News* for the past year!"

He got the information. "Just as I thought–they've raised the rates."

He telephoned Harry Scott, manager of the *News*. "Harry, we had a two-year agreement. What's the meaning of this?"

"Well, there's no contract–no written agreement," answered Scott.

"That's right, Harry, no written agreement, but didn't we have an oral one? Do you deny that?"

"Things change, George. Newsprint costs money. Everything else has gone up as well."

Fuming, George hung up.

Theatres depend on newspapers for building audiences. There were three newspapers in Detroit at the time: the *Free Press,* largely owned by E. D. Stair; the *Times,* a Hearst newspaper; and the *News*.

Because of their dependence on newspapers, the theatre owners and managers of motion-picture houses had formed an organization. A second organization included all theatrical managers, the Detroit Opera House, the Lyceum, the Whitney Opera House and the burlesque houses. The manager of the Cass Theatre was selected to act for the second organization, and George Trendle acted for the motion-picture houses.

George met with the theatre representative and recounted the experience he had had and said, "I believe a fight is in order." Immediately all advertising for motion-picture houses and for the legitimate theatres was taken out of the *News*.

Scott was not a man to run from a fight. He fought back.

He telephoned the theatre owners individually and appealed to them but got nowhere. So he looked for further means of battling.

He decided to call George's action "restraint of trade" and took the matter up with Washington. He named George Trendle as the man behind the action against him. The Washington office sent an officer to the Detroit branch, who decided there was no violation and therefore no cause for action by the *News*.

Harry went along with the decision for a while, but the revenue from theatre advertising is important to a large city newspaper. Moreover, circulation was being affected too. After a while Harry decided that the theatre managers were not going to give in. He telephoned Trendle.

"Why don't you come over and let us talk these things over?"

"No, I don't think so. We've been through all that, and if you want to see me, you can come over here to this office. You're the one who broke the agreement."

Harry hung up. He waited a few more weeks before he called again.

"George, why don't we meet somewhere?"

"Where?"

"The *News* will engage a room at the Statler Hotel. We'll meet and talk."

"All right, but we'll have Dick Lawrence [manager of the Cass Theatre] with us."

The meeting was held, and the *News*, through Harry Scott, agreed to carry the advertising for one more year at the rate previously agreed upon.

Organization of groups was one of George's finest talents, and the financial dealings in which he had a hand were remembered by him to the last little detail.

It was sometime in the twenties that Kunsky and Trendle were asked to join with a group of about forty men—the largest exhibitors in the country—to form a corporation to make motion pictures for its members and others. It was natural to take this step forward. All were exhibitors; they would in the future be producers as well.

The country was split up into forty parts, in each of which a certain theatre owner would have exclusive rights to the marketing of the motion pictures made by the corporation. The whole state of Michigan was allotted to King and Trendle. Trendle was elected to the board of directors with four other men. The five men went to California to buy land on which to build a studio. Richard "Dick" Roland was vice-president and general manager of the corporation, known as First National Pictures, Incorporated. He and George went out to decide on a site. Dick wanted a piece of property on Santa Monica Boulevard. But George felt that a better buy could be made by going through the canyon at Vine Street or nearby. He reasoned that when the road was completed, a car line would be added. This would make an ideal spot. Dick agreed, and they bought, as a starter, twenty acres just beyond the canyon for $20,000, from a farmer. The deal was closed, and the papers were signed by the light of an oil lamp on a kitchen table covered with white oilcloth.

Later the city wanted a corner of this property because of the streetcar lines. An acre and a half was sold to the city for $20,000, so the rest of the property belonged to the organization for nothing. This property, enlarged from time to time, is now owned by Warner Brothers, with one of the largest studios in the world on it.

Dick Roland and George Trendle became quite good friends. Robert Lieber of Indianapolis was president of the organization and Roland vice-president, when some of the forty members, for profit and other reasons, sold some of their stock to Paramount Theatres. Chicago, New Orleans and probably others sold as much as 25 per cent, in some cases perhaps wanting Paramount franchises and having less faith in the solvency of First National.

Talking the situation over, Trendle told Dick, "It won't be long before Paramount can take the whole thing over, and that will be the end of the organization anyway."

Dick agreed. A meeting was held, and the problem came before the entire board. It was decided to sell the remainder of the stock to Warner Brothers for a considerable sum of money. George did not participate in the money—"but it was a good experience."

XIV

For some time George Trendle had had full charge of all the theatres of King-Trendle ownership. They were the Columbia, Alhambra, Garden, Strand, Easttown, Vogue, Alger, Norwest, Birmingham, Ramona, Empress, Adams, Broadway-Capitol, Palms, Michigan United Artists and Fisher. Of these the Fisher was probably most elegant.

On opening night Samuel Benavie conducted the orchestra. Charles Jolley, resplendent in a white satin uniform with gold braid, cut in the style of a Northwest Mountie, sang songs from *Rose Marie*. With him was Marion Roberts Sanborn, a lovely golden-haired leading soprano. The two were tops in Detroit talent.

These were the Roaring Twenties—the age of the flapper—when the telephone number of a good bootlegger could get one "in" anywhere.

In 1924 there were almost 24,000 theatres, museums and music halls in the United States. In this volume sometimes quality slipped away. "Peaches" Browning made the scene. She sued for separation from her husband, "Daddy" Browning, with spectacular disclosures of the details of their marital relationship. With no previous theatrical talent, she appeared on vaudeville stages all over the country.

It was the era which launched Irving Berlin as an exceptional song writer. Years earlier Howard Pierce had written to George from one of the army camps' Liberty Theatres: "There is this young man here, who hangs around the office. He has the worst-fitting uniform I've ever seen, but his songs are pretty good. His singing isn't the best, but I hope we can give him a chance when we get back." He was speaking of Irving Berlin.

In rapid succession came the Florida boom, the discovery

of King Tut's tomb and the Teapot Dome scandal. Contract bridge and the Charleston were born. Great names made the headlines–Gertrude Ederle, "Red" Grange and Charles A. Lindberg, who packed a ham sandwich and some chocolate bars and flew the Atlantic.

In Detroit the Windsor Tunnel and the Ambassador Bridge both opened in the late twenties. It was easier now to get into Canada, where liquor was legal. And Canada obliged by opening its doors and liquor stores. Smuggling took odd forms; wild ingenious devices were invented. The amateurs were frequently caught and fined and the liquor was confiscated. One group went through the customs with regularity, and since they were dressed as nuns and priests drew little attention. But on one such trip a flat tire drew a string of profanity from one of the nuns–in a very masculine voice. The officers took another look!

There were those who made their own liquor, but the cases of poisoning and blindness caused most of the citizens to be extremely chary of this type of liquor. The Volstead Act was a big flop! There are those who believe that drinking actually decreased when the act was repealed.

The twenties roared on. New names came to fame in the entertainment field. Joan Crawford came to Hollywood with large bows on her shoes and made the most of every opportunity there. Jimmy Cagney, George Raft and Milton Berle were three of the newer names.

In Hollywood new-found riches and fame brought a need for new-found play. Parties were extravagant, long-lasting and wild. Stars were surrounded by new friends, hangers-on; the phrase "yes-men" came into being. The "friends" changed as the stars' fortunes changed.

Tragedy struck at one of these parties. A young girl, a guest at the party, was found dead. The most famous name at the party was Roscoe "Fatty" Arbuckle. Fatty, a rotund, happy, funny fellow, became a villain overnight and was tried for murder. He was proved innocent, but the damage to his reputation was irreparable. His pictures became unpopular, no new producer would touch him, and it became known that his fabulous salary had been spent as it arrived and that Fatty was broke.

He went to his former friends for help, but most of them refused. He was eventually to get in touch with Howard O. Pierce. It was perhaps the ridicule of Arbuckle that prompted him to act. In all of his life George had hated ridicule. Now newspapers, vaudevillians and burlesque performers all aimed their jokes at Arbuckle. But no one in any of the King-Trendle theatres. Here the rule was: no poking fun at an audience, no baldhead jokes, no fat-man jokes–no ridicule!

Arbuckle had no friends. Even the persons willing to give him the benefit of the doubt, to grant he could be innocent–even those wanted to steer clear of him. Howard telephoned and talked with Arbuckle directly.

"Is it true?"

"So help me, Howard, I am innocent."

Arbuckle appeared on the stage of the Broadway-Capitol Theatre. He had been given the same publicity, the same production, that any other artist would have been given. His act was advertised simply as "Arbuckle tells his story," and he went on the stage and did just that.

More and more the audience came to sympathize. He finished in a round of applause. Audiences grew during the week. The act was successful in Detroit, and through this booking he was hired for Chicago as well. Curiosity seekers came at first but were convinced the man was innocent. Now, though, the old funny-man magic was gone! The Detroit booking had given but temporary surcease. Still, it gave George and Howard some satisfaction to have tried. Later they had another chance to be helpful to a performer.

"Mr. Trendle, Miss Hopper is on the phone," said the secretary.

"Who is Miss Hopper?" asked George and immediately laughed when he realized it was Edna Wallace Hopper. He had met her in California and in New York, several times. A former star of the Zeigfield Follies, her name was a byword to American theatregoers.

"I am coming through Detroit on my way to the Coast, and if you can find time to see me, I'd like to stop in Detroit."

In a few days she arrived.

"George, I am getting old, and what's more, I show it!"

George demurred politely, "No, Edna."

"I read a mirror well–I've been in this business a long time and I learned that. What's more important, I can read people's faces. People who haven't seen me in a long time are startled at the change. Oh, they don't say so, but they show it."

"I don't see that much of a change, Edna."

"You're being polite but not realistic. The agents don't call me. I'm not getting offers from either the theatre or the films." She hesitated. "I could be through, I guess, but I need money, so if I am through, I have to go down fighting. I am going to California to have my face lifted."

George was doubtful about this new surgical remedy.

"I can't do anything else–but I need your help. When I come back, I want you to agree to give me some spot in one of your theatres–give me a chance to come back."

"All right, use your money to good advantage. Have some film taken before, during, and after the operation. Motion pictures. If you can get some good pictures, come to Detroit on your way back east and we'll put on some morning matinees for women only.

"Before you come out on the platform, we'll show the pictures before and during the operation. Then you appear, and the change will be obvious. You describe the operation while the picture of it is being run. We'll book you 'The Rejuvenation of Edna Wallace Hopper.' "

There had never been a morning matinee. If George had any uneasiness about this innovation, he told no one.

"I know it will be a success," Edna told him on the morning of her first appearance. "You have an instinct about audiences that no one else in the business has. I know it will be all right."

There were lines for more than a block at nine o'clock waiting for the theatre to open at ten. The house was packed for the entire week.

The picture was shown. Edna entered the stage, dressed in a rather short black velvet dress. White lace collar lightened her face, and the outfit was very youthful, but more than that, the face lift had lifted Edna's spirits as well. She was happy! It was contagious! The audience loved her. From this appearance came offers from Chicago. She accepted.

Sometime during this period Edna was approached by a Chicago chemical firm. She was offered 50 per cent in a cosmetic venture if she would allow the use of her name on their new line of beauty preparations. She accepted and almost immediately became a very wealthy woman.

"It is all due to your faith in me," she telephoned George from New York. "Now I have asked a writer to do my biography. I think women of America have proved through their acceptance of my theatre act and the cosmetics that they have an interest in me. You were the person who gave me my start on the comeback trail, and so I'd like to put you in my book."

An interview took place between the writer and George. A chapter was written and approved. The book was never completed. Edna Wallace Hopper died suddenly.

XV

George W. Trendle was a master at organization. Over and over this was proved.

Organizing for bargaining and strength was a comparatively new thing in labor, however. Now it began. These were times when employers wondered, "Where will this end? If they gain a little, then what? Will they want to take over?"

Now came the organization of the motion-picture operators who had charge of the projection of pictures from the small rooms in which they sat, hour after hour. They felt that with organization they would make more money and have better hours and some fringe benefits besides. It was while the bargaining was going on between the management and the operators that one night, after the theatre had closed, a bomb was exploded in the side exit of the State Theatre. At the same time, although George was not directly negotiating with the operators, several threatening letters were received at his home, which frightened his wife.

Patronage dropped off at the State Theatre, and George knew something would have to be done. While he was contemplating his course of action, more letters arrived. George feared for the safety of his family. He took his troubles to Bert Brown, head of the United States Secret Service in Detroit.

Brown told him, "I do have some contacts with undercover gangsters. It looks as if they may be in this thing."

Trendle looked surprised.

"Oh, it's all in the course of my work. Such contacts are necessary. They can give me a lot of useful information"—he smiled ruefully—"that is, if I don't double-cross them."

"Then you think you can help?"

"I handle forgery and bank thefts only, but if you wish I will make arrangements for you to see a man who has connection with the underworld." Then he went on, "He won't be responsible for this, but he may know someone who can be helpful."

"Who is he?"

"No names, George. Call him Joe Doakes."

Somehow the trouble stopped at once, and the negotiations with the organized operators went on smoothly. At the same time "Joe" told his troubles to George! He was, he said, being picked up all the time. "This is stupid and downright inconvenient. . . . I am not breaking any Detroit laws. What I am doing is running an organization to protect the Mississippi River steamboat gamblers from hijackers."

George arranged a meeting for Joe with Police Commissioner Rutledge, and Joe called on George in his office and thanked him. "I'm all right with the cops now. But if I can ever do anything more for you, just let me know." And George considered the matter closed.

The letters had frightened his wife, and she wondered if they should take the steps some of their friends had taken and employ bodyguards for their children or send them away. But George said, "No." He wanted his children at home with him, and bodyguards were unthinkable.

It was during the mid-twenties that the crumbling of their marriage was making itself evident. Kathryn's sister lived with the couple, and more and more the two sisters withdrew from his life. There was a wide variance of tastes and differences in their requirements from life. Neither George nor his wife was happy. It was recognized by both that this marriage was born of propinquity; but it had brought to them the two children: George Washington, Jr., a fine, sturdy bright boy of ten, and Mary Kathryn, as pretty and as dainty as a Dresden doll.

The parents talked the situation over. In the cold light of reality, with calm decisiveness and with no recriminations, they decided that they would stay together until the children were old enough to leave for schools away from home and then would get a divorce.

During this period George spent as much time as his busy schedule would allow with his children. Years before, he had bought property on the shore of Lake Erie, east of Cleveland, and there he built a gray-shingled cottage. Friday night of each weekend he would take the Cleveland boat to Cleveland, where he was picked up by car and taken to the cottage. The children loved the cottage and looked forward to the closing of school for this important reason: it would be time to go to the cottage.

George had established a fine relationship with his children. He and his son "talked things over." And Mary K. was the light of his life and knew it. From the harshness of the business world to the soft appeal of the little girl was wonderful surcease for George.

Both children inherited their father's fine imagination. Both reveled in his presence, and both loved his story-telling ability. He would begin in various ways, but usually it was the story of the pet who lived only in his imagination as a child.

"It was while I had my fine pet, the elephant. I used to ride on his back. But you know how high an elephant is; so my elephant used to kneel down and put his trunk way out straight in front of him and I would walk up his trunk and take my place right at the back of his neck.

"One fine day I walked up his trunk as usual, and lo and behold! there, sitting as if he owned the world, was a big, big lion!

"Naturally I was surprised, but I wasn't very frightened because I knew the elephant would dispose of him if he became unfriendly. Besides, no one I knew had a lion and an elephant, so I wanted to keep him. I just sat down beside him.

"Off we went for our swim in the Detroit River. Down past the Eastern market we went, and Jumbo swiped a carrot as we passed the farmer's stall, past the old church on Jefferson, then out Jefferson Avenue to the north side of the river opposite the Belle Isle bathhouse! People stared and stared, but we went about our business.

"Now, I had a problem. Oh, your grandmother might put up with an elephant, but a real live lion—never."

Here Mary K. would show her concern for the poor homeless lion, and her father quickly ended the story on a happier note.

"We swam up and down the Detroit River, past the yacht club, past the Edison plant with the seven smokestacks, past the little sailboats and the big freighters that bring the iron ore from Upper Michigan. I was worried that I might just have to push the lion off, and we were going past Belle Isle again, when suddenly out of the woods the prettiest lady lion you ever saw darted out of the woods and swished her tail and batted her eyelashes at us. My fine big new friend just jumped off Jumbo's back and swam for shore."

"Did he ever come back?"

"Never; and I didn't find out whether the lady lion took him in as a friend, a son, a love or whatever. Now, maybe when you go to the zoo at Belle Isle you will look for them both. She was cute, but he was kind of a scraggly old lion with a mean old face, except when he smiled—as he did at the lady lion. It was a pretty nice smile—that is, if you care for lion's smiles."

George junior was a bit old to be too gullible. He would wink at his father and say, "Let's get in the lake before it gets dark."

Mary K. said, "I'll go, too—we can play."

George junior said, "We want to swim"; then, at Mary's disappointed look, "Dad can be the elephant–I'll be him as a little boy."

"What about me?" wailed his sister.

"You be the lady lion and come out of the bushes as we go by."

Years later, when George told a story which sounded unlikely to his daughter, she would say, eyes twinkling, "Another elephant?"

The weekends were a fine rest and rejuvenator for George. During the week he was more and more busy as time went by. His partner, King, lost interest in the theatres. "You run them, George," he would say and go back to northern Michigan to a resort hotel which he had built up there.

The summer, too, was a time when George saw more of his mother and sisters. His mother lived with Clara, and they were near enough to his home on LaSalle Boulevard so that he could see them quite often.

Not far away his sister Jen and her husband, Mark, lived, and they could keep an eye on his mother while he was away on weekends. They remained a close family.

XVI

MOTION PICTURES WERE GOING GREAT, and there was now much talk of adding sound to the pictures. As early as 1907 a process called Chromophone presented film in color with sound synchronized. But the system was unsatisfactory, and the experiment failed. Later a process called Cameraphone involving the use of Victrola records was tried. Even a combination of the two systems was tried.

A well-known actress in the play *Camille* used to stop the running of the film and do the death scene in person.

George was coming home from Washington one night, by train. He went into the club car as usual, carrying papers that he wanted to go over. At about ten o'clock he started back to his own car and couldn't find it. The conductor admitted when questioned that while George was in the club car, the train had been split and the other section was following about one hour behind this section. It had been announced through the train, but he was not sure it had been announced in the club car.

George was furious. All his luggage, even his overcoat, for it was late fall, was in the other section.

"We'll drop you at the switch shanty, and the train will stop for you."

The switch shanty was cold. The small oil stove gave off insufficient heat, and the oil lamp sputtered. Between them they gave off an odor, and George, his hat, coat and luggage an hour away, was incensed. He had his briefcase under his arm but didn't open it. Instead he huddled against the wall, and his mind went back to the inconsequential talk with friends in Washington. Someone had remarked, "Someday we'll have talking pictures–they're bound to come."

When the second section of the train arrived and stopped

and George got on, everyone in the car was surprised. More imaginative minds had pictured him pushed off the train, or falling off, and since the conductor who knew the whole story was on the train ahead, no one knew where he had been. George was sure he must contract a cold or pneumonia, but actually nothing happened, except that a plan for talking pictures had been conceived. Sitting there in the switch shanty, huddling against the cold, he had dreamed up a way.

"Howard," he said to Pierce, "tell me what you think of this idea for talking pictures!" And he related his plan. To Pierce, who was in his glory producing illusory effects, it was a real challenge.

At the Lafayette Theatre a long platform was constructed about three feet off the floor, behind the screen. Actors and actresses were hired with voices which should fit the parts on the screen. They would walk back and forth on the platform and speak the words which the characters on the screen were supposed to be saying. Screens were lightweight, and the picture could be seen from the back of the screen as well as from the front. The illusion was very effective.

They were advertised as "talking pictures"—and they really were, because actors and actresses were actually talking. There was no machine to desynchronize or run behind. The system was an immediate success. George and Howard were elated. It looked like the beginning of a very successful run—except for one thing!

Soon afterward Warner Brothers made a talking picture with the sound on a flat disc, starring Al Jolson and titled *The Jazz Singer*. It was intended to carry just songs, but sometime during the filming, as the songs were being recorded, Jolson looked up in response to a compliment and said, "Hold it, you ain't heard nothing yet." It was such a natural ad-lib that it was decided to leave it in and to add to it with some dialogue between Jolson and the actress playing his mother.

The picture was a sensation. George wanted it. The rate of $25,000 a week was $10,000 over the usual fee. He wanted it for the Adams but not at Warner's price, and he began to dicker.

The bargaining lever was a slight one–the picture was too popular for bargain pricing–but he did arrive at a figure below the original price by offering a percentage and by having the picture run as long as it was popular, at the Adams. *The Jazz Singer* ran for ten weeks. Warner collected $28,000, but the advertising was wonderful for them. Exhibitors came from every section of the country to see it and ask questions.

In pictures *The Jazz Singer* was the start of a new era. Big names now were culled from the vaudeville stage but just as often names quite unknown previously. Some of the former silent stars had voices totally unsuited to the new medium. John Gilbert, Lon Chaney, Charlie Chaplin and Harold Lloyd were some of these. New names appeared on the marquees. The Marx Brothers, Bob Hope, Bing Crosby and George Jessel were among the newcomers.

Never was such enthusiastic acceptance known in the motion-picture world! George felt this excitement for a little while, but as usual, when he had accomplished success in one line, he began to reach for new fields. His satisfaction came from planning and executing the plans. The finished product was not as exciting as the process of arriving at it.

Some time later, on leaving the Broadway-Capitol Theatre with his friend Howard O. Pierce, and crossing Madison Avenue, Trendle asked, "What do you think of radio, Howard?"

"Radio? I haven't thought much about it–not yet."

"Well, we'd better start thinking of something, Howard. Have you read *Variety* this morning?"

"Every morning, George–I read *Variety* the instant it comes to me. And let me tell you, the headlines today are no comfort to me. Out of more than five thousand vaudeville acts, only about five hundred are working," said Pierce. "It's not as tough getting acts now, but I don't like it."

Trendle nodded, and the two men walked on. The discussion turned to other topics, but it wasn't long before both men had cause to remember the conversation. As Trendle suspected, a depression was in the making.

Exhibitors had agreements in the various sections of the country not to invade one another's territory. One of the most effective of these had been between the King-Trendle interests and Balaban and Katz; the latter's headquarters were in Chicago. Now, however, Balaban and Katz had made a deal to build the Michigan Theatre in Detroit.

It was contrary to the agreement, and George Trendle called a meeting of the First National Pictures Association in Atlantic City. Barney Balaban said that Sam Katz had made the deal without his consent or knowledge. Negotiations began, and the King-Trendle interests offered Babalban and Katz a 25 per cent interest in their entire chain of theatres in Detroit if Balaban and Katz would finish the Michigan Theatre and turn it over to the King-Trendle interests, known officially as the United Detroit Theatres Corporation, to be managed by them. Neither party was particularly pleased with a deal of this kind; nevertheless, negotiations were started.

It was agreed by all parties that Sidney Kent, president of Paramount Pictures, would be the arbitrator. At length, after listening to both sides, he said, "Barney, your partner made a deal to stay out of Detroit. It's a fair deal; take 25 per cent and get out. Be glad to get it." Sidney was curt.

George called Sam Katz. "Haven't you had enough of this fooling around, Sam?"

Sam sputtered and fumbled, and it was evident to George that Sam's end of the conversation was being monitored–his conversation was stilted. But he ended by saying, "Okay,

George," and the theatre was turned over to King-Trendle, who didn't want the competition.

But Katz was not in the least mollified actually. He tried it all over again, with the United Artists Theatre. Again he was called to order, and again he tried to put the blame on his partner. And again he telephoned Trendle and asked, "Would you like to have the United Artists Theatre?"

"Not at all," came the response. "The rent is too high, and the operation is unprofitable. Isn't that true?"

"I don't want any trouble with you, George. We've been friends a long time, and I'd like to continue as friends. You know the Detroit audiences better than anyone, and I am sure you could make a go of it."

George was tired of the competition, but he thought he could not make a go of it because of the excessive rent. He knew there were other considerations causing Katz to try to get out of the deal, but he didn't mention them. He felt that Katz was trying for the presidency of Paramount Pictures Corporation. Adolph Zukor was president, and Sam did not want Zukor to know that he, Sam Katz, had incurred the ill will of one of the largest exhibitors in the country and he made still another offer when they disagreed regarding the United Artists Theatre. "Would you be interested in selling the Detroit theatres?"

George talked with his partner. "Mr. King, this might be just the right time to get out of the business. Perhaps it is the best time to sell out."

But King was reluctant. "We've got a good thing going, George. Why change anything now?"

But George wanted to sell out and get his 25 percent in cash. He urged King to accept.

Finally, "All right, George, but this combination–you and me–it's too good to break up. I'll sell if you'll agree to find something else for us to do together."

George agreed, and together they left for New York.

Now, however, a dissident stockholder had filed a suit for an injunction which would restrain Paramount from buying the theatres, and it became a question of avoiding the serving of the injunction. The Paramount attorney met the two men at the train and took them up a back stairs to a dressing room of the Paramount Theatre.

The Paramount attorney suggested that the Detroit men take stock in Paramount. It was selling for $75 a share at the time. George held out for a cash deal. The money involved was something over $4,000,000, which was paid one half in cash and the other half held in notes to be paid at the rate of $20,000 a week.

When it was all agreed and the papers were properly signed, John H. King turned to George and asked, "What now, George? You promised to go into something else with me."

"I'm looking around," said George.

The Detroit *News* said in part, "Trendle's career as a motion picture impressario dates back to the first faint beginnings of the old silent days. . . . One of the early promoters of a business that seemed at the time to have scant possibilities but which subsequently rewarded the faith of the promoters with handsome returns. . . . When the first sale of stock in the early motion pictures began it was the young lawyer, Trendle, who was asked to take charge. He made good completely."

The *News* went on: "A civic minded man, George Trendle was appointed to the Detroit Board of Fire Commissioners in 1925. In 1928 he became president for one term. He was president five times the 23 years he served. At present he is still serving on the Board."

The Detroit *Free Press* wrote: "The resignation of George W. Trendle as president and executive head of the United Theatres Corporation, in order to take care of the growth of other interests, is a matter of real regret among the patrons of the motion picture theatres in Detroit.

"Controlling several large downtown theatres and a number of houses in other parts of the city, Mr. Trendle has maintained standards which have been a genuine credit to the community and a satisfaction to audiences.

"Mr. Trendle has stood for cleanliness, morality, wholesome atmosphere and entertainment of the highest grade obtainable. When necessary, he carried the fight for these things as far as Hollywood itself.

"Mr. Trendle has been a credit to the entertainment business and he is needed."

The *Free Press* was right. George Trendle watched every picture for objectionable material. Howard Pierce watched every vaudeville act–as did George. When in doubt, George said, "It is better to err on the right side." Sometimes this editing and censoring verged on the comical.

Long before the sale of the theatres, Earl Carrol's *Vanities*, playing in Cleveland, was advertised as the finest in showmanship. And George wanted the finest for the Michigan Theatre. So Howard Pierce went down to Cleveland to see the act. He reported by telephone that it was a very beautiful act, but knowing George's stand on decency, he said, "There's a good bit of nudity."

"Engage the act," said George. "We'll dress them up." The Michigan had always been advertised as "family-type entertainment." The director, the actors and actresses, in fact the whole company, were furious when they learned they were expected to wear clothes in the act. But George was adamant–tights, skirts, and so forth were found, and the company was clothed.

The press caught the story. The headlines on the theatre pages read, "Trendle dresses the Vanities" and played it up big! Oddly enough, the publicity which could have been disastrous turned out to be very good indeed for the theatre. The public turned out in large numbers to view the *Vanities* in clothes.

There was legislation in several cities which banned the "show of flesh." Boston led the fight in legislation, but Boston went too far, and some of the best publicity a show could have was "Banned in Boston."

Detroit, with George Trendle in a leading role, had its own set of rules. He felt strongly about the presentation of wholesome entertainment. Ribald gags were cut out of acts, and if the actor objected, his own run was cut short. George had his own set of rules. He felt the responsibility of the entertainment world to the young people. He watched their shows sharply.

He watched that no one segment of the audience should feel ridicule–no spotlights on baldheads, no remarks to specific groups of people in the audience, no suggestive language or actions.

Since he also was a director on the board of First National Pictures, he had some influence in the making of films, and it is true that he "carried," as the *Free Press* said, "the fight all the way to Hollywood."

It was not all work and no play, however, and George came to know socially and professionally many of the Hollywood greats.

King never went along if he could avoid it. More and more he was involved with the North Michigan venture into the resort business, and he spent less and less time in Detroit.

"What kind of man was John H. King?"

George answered, "Mr. King was what I call, sincerely, an honest businessman. He had quit school at the age of ten or eleven and gone to work in some factory or other. He wound up at Caille Motor Company. He saved his money and invested it wisely. When the opportunity came for John H. King to go into business for himself, he was ready!

"You never needed anything in writing from Mr. King. If he gave his word, you didn't need anything more–no written contract with him. His word was enough. To my knowledge, he never cheated a soul of anything. From the time I started with him, he let me run things to suit myself. He knew that in order to get the best of my effort, he had to keep Arthur Caille off my neck. And this he did.

"I think he saw something in me that I didn't see myself. He was satisfied. He trusted me implicitly. When I placed papers before him, with the 'x' where he should sign, he didn't question me–he signed."

Now King was asking with some eagerness, "What now, George? Where do we go from here?"

XVII

KING DID NOT GO BACK to northern Michigan at once. He stayed around Detroit, coming into his office every day, waiting, expectant for a next move.

"Well"—King looked up from his desk at George, who was speaking—"what you think of our going into radio?"

"Oh, now, George, that's a new thing. Hardly anyone is making any real money in it—"

"Some people are. But I'll tell you what I think about it. Radio is 'something for nothing.' The public is very interested. Think of it—once a set is bought, you can sit in your own home and hear anything from prize fights to grand opera!"

King looked skeptical, but he nodded in reluctant agreement. Then he said, "But you gotta be good!"

"We've had years of stage productions behind us. We know how to be good!"

Something for nothing! That was radio. Free entertainment. And George was right—the American public picked it up very readily.

What sort of programs? Every sort! Prize fights—the Dempsey-Firpo fight, election returns, even hypnotism. For a hypnotist in Kansas City put a young lady to sleep on the stage of a local theatre while he stayed in the radio station four blocks away.

Amateurs had a field day, for many stations had little funds to pay professionals. In 1925 there were more than five hundred stations in operation. And many fell by the wayside. It was an expensive experiment, but as some fell more came into the picture, and the industry was launched.

Because vaudeville was, as an industry, slowing up considerably, some of the actors and actresses would appear for the publicity alone. Others refused to join, thinking they were competing against themselves.

Radio began to sell time to sponsors–later, talent. And talent began to demand more than just publicity, and to get it. Suddenly there was a rush to be included. Will Rogers said, "Radio is too big a thing to be out of." In rapid succession Jeanette MacDonald, Nelson Eddy, José Iturbi, Lily Pons, Robert Merrill and Jan Pierce, as well as countless others, entered the field as performers.

Tex Rickard built a radio station atop Madison Square Garden for the express purpose of broadcasting his fights.

In 1928 the Dodge Brothers paid $60,000 for one hour of broadcasting, and the radio audience was of such importance to Dodge that the studio doors were locked and no studio audience was allowed at all. The "Festival of Stars" included Norma Talmadge, Dolores Del Rio, Douglas Fairbanks, John Barrymore, D. W. Griffith and Paul Whiteman. It is said that Charles Chaplin was there but that he froze with mike fright. On a later show Al Jolson and Fred Stone appeared.

In early 1929, Walter Winchell sent out a flash that he was going on the air with a forty-two-station hookup. American Telephone and Telegraph supplied the facilities at what was then considered an enormous rate. And *Variety* reported, "Radio is here to stay."

A new industry was to George a new opportunity. He read the trade papers with renewed interest, looking for an opportunity. *Variety* was known as the show people's bible but at this time carried a different story entirely. "Wall Street Lays an Egg" headlined *Variety* in October, 1929. The stock-market crash, on famous Black Tuesday, was heard round the world.

When the Detroit theatres were sold by King-Trendle and George had insisted on cash and notes, no stock, he was wiser than even he suspected. Now the former theatre owners

George W. Trendle at the age of five, with his brother Carl.

Trendle when he graduated law school, 1908.

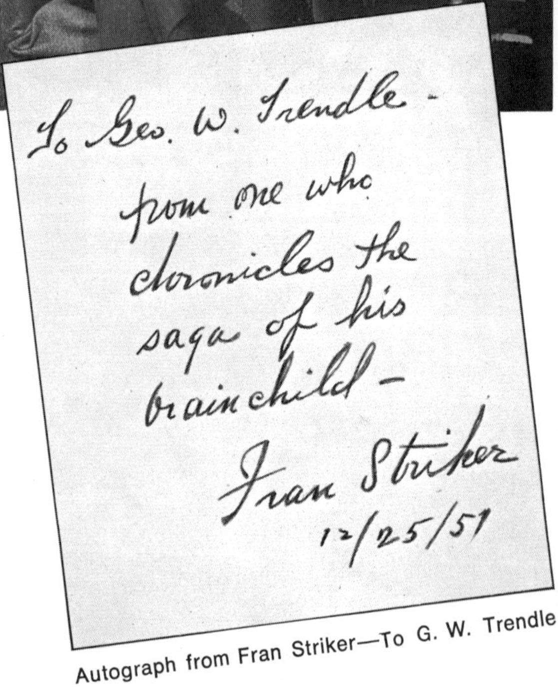

To Geo. W. Trendle -
from one who
chronicles the
saga of his
brainchild -
Fran Striker
12/25/51

Autograph from Fran Striker—To G. W. Trendle

Brace Beamer, Fran Striker, George Trendle, Allen Campbell and Charles Livingstone.

Recent photo of H. Allen Campbell.

Raymond J. Meurer.

Howard O. Pierce.

Sergeant Preston of the Yukon and the dog, Yukon King.

Hi Yo Silver.

Britt Reid as
The Green Hornet.

Britt Reid as himself.

Mrs. Dwight Johnson, Mr. Trendle's daughter, now residing in San Diego, California.

Mr. Trendle's son, George W. Trendle, Jr., now living in Honolulu, Hawaii.

Mr. and Mrs. Trendle.

George W. Trendle.

throughout the country who had accepted Paramount stock in payment began to question one another and themselves. For Paramount stock, at the time it was offered to George, was $75 a share, but when the smoke began to clear after the market crash, a sorry bunch of stockholders noted that Paramount now was selling for $13 a share!

King noticed the market price of Paramount stock and said, "You did a good job, there, George." "Is this praise or a nudge to go ahead and find a new business?" wondered George.

He heard that a Detroit radio station might be for sale. It was station WGHP, owned by George Harrison Phelps. Phelps, successful in the advertising industry, wanted to get out of radio. So the station passed into other hands, those of Mr. Storer of Storer Broadcasting Company.

Arriving at a financial setup for the station corporation was another matter. King wanted a straight partnership with George, but George wanted his friend Howard O. Pierce to have a part in the new venture. He set it up so that King and he each took 40 per cent of the stock and Pierce took the remaining 20 per cent. He then drew up the purchase agreement, and the station was bought for $250,000.

Later he said, "I made a boo-boo." A stipulation which read that Storer could not own a radio station in the United States within ninety miles of Detroit for a period of five years did not mention Canada. Windsor, Ontario, is right across the Detroit River from Detroit, and in a short time broadcasting was heard from a new station owned by Storer in Windsor. George telephoned Storer; the details of the conversation were never disclosed, but shortly after the conversation the Canadian station was closed.

After the five-year period had elapsed, Storer opened station WJBK. He was a fine competitor, and the two men remained friendly.

Call letters for a station are important in the sense that they must be easily identifiable in the listener's mind, and George hit upon "WXYZ–the last thing in radio." In order to use these call letters, he had to have the approval and permission of the United States Navy and Army. At the moment these were being held in reserve.

The situation constituted a challenge for George Trendle. He liked the slogan "the last thing in radio," and he had to have those call letters.

First he called on the Army Communications Department. He was told, "You don't have a chance–the Navy would never relinquish those call letters."

"Would you be willing to relinquish the letters if I can get Navy permission?"

"I don't see why not. But I am sure you cannot get the Navy permission."

It was enough for George. He went to the Navy with the same story and was given, practically word for word, the same assurance. "If you can get Army permission, we will go along. But we are sure that you will never get Army permission."

Without telling the Navy officer that he had the Army commitment, George asked for a letter to that effect, which he was given without hesitation.

Back to the Army with the Navy letter, and George was given permission by the Army to use the call letters. He attached both letters to his application to the Federal Communications Commission, and his application was accepted. Success! And success in other fields, as well!

George had become a millionaire! His dream had come true. He had as a boy dreamed of being a millionaire, and he had hoped, as part of that dream, to be useful to his fellow man. Now he had assets of far more than a million dollars, and he had facilities to be useful beyond his childhood dreams –the means to supply the youth of the nation with inspiration, with an ideal to follow. Two dreams had come true. He should have been a very happy man.

But George was lonely. By the very nature of his position, in his company, in his work, he had to stand alone. Like the point of an arrow, the head man in any industry stands alone. There were many would-be confidants, but decisions had to be made, in the final analysis, by him and the consequences borne by him.

At home his wife and her sister had interests which excluded him. Kathryn was a homebody. Safe in the comfort of home and family, she had no desire to mingle with the outside world. There grew to be such a disparity of interests between the two that nothing could bridge it. Mutually they had agreed years before on divorce. And now George made his application—or rather, allowed Kathryn to make hers.

About the loneliness he would do something. His children were grown and in college. He needed an outside interest, preferably in athletics.

He stopped at a riding academy on Hamilton Avenue and inquired about riding lessons. "Three dollars per lesson or fifty dollars for a full course of twenty-five lessons," he was told.

"I'll take it," said George—"the full course, I mean. I hope I can stick it out. But if I should want to quit, don't give me my money back. If you refuse a refund, I think I will finish the series."

The first lesson was torture. George, who had never been on a horse, even as a child, felt as if he were on the peak of a mountain. This sport was completely alien to him. He went to the academy owner and told him so. Said the owner, "Remember your bargain. No refunds! I think you are just going through beginner's quakes. You are really doing quite well. You'll be all right." And he was. George became a good, not spectacular, rider. He joined the Detroit Riding and Hunt

Club. And he might have been an expert, but he never had the time or the inclination to make friends with his horse.

He bought his first horse from Charles T. Fisher and got his first taste of *caveat emptor*. He left the bridal path one morning and tried to ride a bit of cross country. The horse stepped into a slight hole, stumbled and tossed his rider over his head. Luckily no bones were broken in either George or the horse.

Back in the stable George learned that this horse had been trained entirely on smooth footing and could not adjust to uneven ground. No time was lost in an exchange of horses. The new one looked the same to George–a big brown horse. He never had time to cultivate a horse, and one looked the same as another to him. "Is this my horse?" he would ask when the horse was brought to him. This furnished much amusement to the other riders, and they would kid him about it.

He finally bought a fine black horse–"a magnificent animal about seventeen hands high with four white socks which came halfway up to his knees. There were little black spots on the white socks. "No one could miss this horse," said George. "He was beautiful." At last George was describing his own horse. He had established rapport with him and was now at home riding, cross country or in the ring at the club.

His hours for business had long been the afternoon and evening, so that he had his mornings open for riding. There were, too, the Sunday-morning breakfast rides, a stiff cross-country ride. The riders were divided according to ability. As they returned to the club some of the riders would take the jumps, which were alongside the gates, while the less experienced would stand aside until the hurdles were taken and wait to have the gates opened by an attendant.

One of the more experienced riders was a tiny brown-haired, brown-eyed woman who rode with her daughter almost every morning. She sailed over the hurdles. And George noticed how she sat her horse and how she handled the animal as if she had ridden all her life, as indeed she had. At first George admired her skill in horsemanship; then admiration became friendship, and soon they were leading the Wednesday-night music rides together.

Chosen for skill and appearance to lead, they were a most elegant-looking pair. A year or two after George's divorce was granted, he and Adelaide Lloyd Huston were married.

Of this marriage, George said, "Adelaide and I have had a very nice life together. We have enjoyed all of the same things–swimming, riding and dancing." The riding was stopped some years later when the doctor told George that the constant jolting had worn the discs of his spine thin.

"Find another hobby," said the doctor. "It is natural with age to have the discs wear thin, so it's advisable to avoid any additional strain." The couple took up bicycling. Sometimes, as they rode together on the shore of Lake Saint Clair where they lived, George recalled his first bike riding.

He was ten or eleven, and his father had bought for himself, as a means of getting to and from work, a used bicycle. As he did with most of his belongings, the father took excellent care of the bicycle. He painted it and polished it.

Since his work was at night, he slept during the day, and the bicycle was parked at the back of the house, a great temptation to the young lad.

One day, as his mother shopped for groceries, George rolled the bicycle over to the fence and mounted. The street was unpaved, the wooden sidewalk was about a foot off the ground, and the boy rode the bicycle on the sidewalk, wobbling from side to side and quite aware of the danger of falling off.

The Eastern Market was about six blocks away and an ideal spot for practicing, since the huge space was filled with farmers' wagons during the morning but quite empty in the afternoon. George rode round and round for about an hour and then back home. There was his father, leaning against the fence.

"Young man, what are you doing with my bicycle?"

George hung his head, fearing the worst. "I shouldn't have done it."

"Where did you go?"

George told him. "I know I should have asked you, but you were asleep and I didn't want to waken you."

"You say you rode on the sidewalk all the way?"

"Yes, Dad."

"You're smarter than I thought. Next time you will ask permission. But if you scratch it or break it, you'll be in a hell of a mess."

Later he heard his father telling, "You know, Mother, that kid can ride as well as I do."

But the challenge was gone. And George rarely asked for his father's bicycle.

XVIII

"MR. TRENDLE, A MR. STAIR wants to talk to you. He called twice and left word for you to call."

"I wonder what he wants now," thought George. It was the same Stair who had refused to confirm his predecessor's commitment for the loan for the building of the Broadway-Capitol Theatre and the same Stair who had bought the bonds on the same building and kept them until maturity. He telephoned Stair.

"Hello, George," said Mr. Stair, as if they had just seen each other the day before. "If you are going to be in this neighborhood, I wish you'd drop in and see me."

"Just like that," thought George, but aloud he said, "all right, I'll do that, and if you happen to be up here in my neighborhood, you drop in to see me."

In a few days they had a conversation, and it went something like this:

"George, I have been thinking of selling the *Free Press*." George was amazed. Stair and the *Free Press* were synonymous. Stair went on, "I have watched the way you conduct your own business, and I think you are just the person I'd like to have the paper go to."

George hid his amazement and his pleasure at the compliment. "How much money is involved?" he asked.

"I'd like to keep the building, keep the machinery and rent the entire outfit to you. It's worth somewhere in the vicinity of five million dollars."

"I asked how much money is involved."

"So you did, George—so you did. Well, I'm not trying to evade the question. I'd have to have a good down payment on the lease to guarantee that you're really interested." In a moment he went on, "This is no idle offer. As I said, I have investigated you thoroughly. I am willing to make a deal that will be profitable to you in the long run.

"I've watched you over the years, I know you could make a success of the paper."

George left the building both flattered and flabbergasted.

He had a young friend, Cliff Prevost, whom he had engaged to do some writing for him. Cliff was in Washington at the time working for the *Free Press* as their Washington correspondent. He had been a reporter at City Hall in Detroit and had written a radio show for WXYZ called "Town Talk." Officials who were not doing their jobs well were frequently blasted in the program. Cliff was a good man, and George trusted him.

George telephoned him. "What I really need, Cliff, is someone with a half million dollars to put into this thing. Mr. King and I are involved in so many other things that I don't want to tie us up on this one."

In a few days Cliff called back. "Mr. Trendle, I have your man."

"Good. What's his name?"

"It's Jim Farley, George. Does that surprise you?"

"Not so much. A Detroit paper would be a big help to Mr. Farley. But I'll have to think that one over, Cliff."

Jim Farley was a big Democratic figure in New York State, particularly in the days of Al Smith and later on, Franklin D. Roosevelt. George went back to Stair.

"Mr. Stair, I have the money man, but I'm not sure you will like the idea."

When he learned the identity of the person willing to put up half a million dollars, Stair said, "No, George, this paper is a Republican paper. I want it to remain a Republican paper. Why don't you look further?"

Then George mulled over the possibility of owning a newspaper himself, and the responsibility. He knew that in taking over a newspaper he would be taking a bigger gamble than he had heretofore engaged in. He decided against it. At first Mr. Stair was reluctant to believe him, but he seemed even more disappointed. He loved his newspaper, and he wanted it in hands that he chose.

In a sense Trendle was relieved. Divested of his responsibility in the motion-picture field and knowing that running a newspaper would not be his job either, he would do what he had been doing–a good job with the radio station. A love of work, he thought, was a genuine blessing.

As a child, under his mother's guidance, it had been his ambition to become a preacher. He hadn't figured which church would benefit from his effort, but he was sure that he wanted to be useful to his fellow man. Later, when he changed to law, he retained his idea of being helpful in some manner to the youth of America. Then, when he went into the motion-picture field in management, he personally screened most of the pictures. He watched for violence, smut and "adverse emotional influence." He still had the urge to be "useful."

Now he thought that he might go into the political world. His income was sufficient, and his financial status was strong. He took stock: his net worth was about $3,000,000. And it was all well invested. He had more than 1,500 shares of the Union Guardian Bank Group stock which he had received because of a series of bank consolidations and an initial investment of $100,000. This stock was now worth between $600 and $900 a share. He had established a very large trust fund as well. He began to think of selling these assets, investing in non-taxables and living comfortably with his family for the rest of his life.

For a boy who began life with few advantages–handicapped by ignorance of his country's language–he had come a long way. He could quit, but he had to have some worthwhile activity–he had to "serve." And he thought he might run for United States senator. Political friends advised him that he would have little trouble unseating the incumbent James Couzens. Radio station WXYZ would assure him a fair shake in publicity.

He knew he was set up to do a good job. The plan was almost complete, when fate intervened. Nietzsche wrote, "Our destiny exercises its influence even when, as yet, we have not learned its nature."

When *Variety* published "Wall Street Lays an Egg," no one knew or even guessed how big an egg and how bad. Even the experts did not guess the bad effects of that day in October, 1929.

General Motors stock was selling for $72 one day. Two weeks later it was going for $7⅝. The Great Depression was on its way. The flood of selling that began in October went on, intensified, until about November 13 and then leveled off. Meanwhile great fortunes went down the drain. Some investors, shocked by the turn of events, stood by numbed and simply watched their life savings dwindle.

The banks were in trouble. In Detroit the Union Guardian Group needed something like $43,000,000 to keep from going under. The Reconstruction Finance Company, newly formed under President Hoover, had already loaned the Chicago banks something like $90,000,000. It was felt in some circles that there was little likelihood of a refusal to the Detroit banks.

An old personal feud between Henry Ford and James Couzens came to light when Senator Couzens said there was no reason for such a large loan to the Detroit banks if Henry Ford would come forward. He could, said Couzens, subordinate his deposits of $25,000,000. Ford refused.

There might have been some merit to Couzens' proposal if he were dealing with his own money. There had been a similar situation in 1895, when the government found its gold deposits slipping away and desperately needed money with which to buy gold to underwrite or buttress its currency. The President turned to J. Pierpont Morgan.

Morgan had the financial prestige to assure bankers and men of means that they could with safety lend money to their government. The banks were saved.

Twelve years later there was a bank panic which centered in New York. Again Morgan came to the rescue. He bullied wealthy men to come to the rescue for the New York banks, and once again the storm was weathered.

But not so in Detroit, in 1932. Governor Comstock, hoping to clear the air, declared a bank holiday, which was to last for one week. Weeks and months passed, and with few exceptions all the banks in the nation were closed.

Embittered depositors quarreled, placing blame here or there, verbal brickbats flew, and eventually there was a congressional investigation. After seven or eight months the committee decided that no one person or industry was to blame. The bank trials ended.

Trendle took stock again of his own financial position. Before Governor Comstock's ill-advised bank holiday, the 1,547 shares of bank stock had been worth from \$600 to \$900 each. Now the stock was less than worthless, for each share had an assessment of \$10 against it. A total of \$15,470 was due on the shares. All in all, Trendle's net worth had dropped from close to \$3,000,000 to less than \$750,000, of which \$500,000 was tied up in a trust fund to insure payments of alimony to his former wife.

"Politics will have to wait," said Trendle to his associates. "I am about to start all over again."

Between 1929 and 1932, when stocks fell more than 60 per cent and American industry was operating at less than half its former levels, the theatres suffered proportionately more than any other business.

In Detroit the new management was trying desperately to make the theatres a profitable undertaking once more. Prospective customers were lured with offers of free dishes, free tickets, free coffee, free gum, but all this effort failed to bring back the customers in their former numbers.

The theatres were thrown into receivership, and S. A. Lynch of Atlanta was appointed receiver. He launched an investigation, and at the end of it he was convinced that there was one man who could save the theatres in Detroit and that man was George W. Trendle.

The year the theatres were sold, the profit, under Trendle's management, was about $945,000. Both men knew this. Lynch knew that if anyone could bring the theatres back to a profitable undertaking, Trendle was the person to do it. Lynch came to Detroit and telephoned Trendle.

Trendle wanted the job–and Lynch wanted Trendle for the job. Each wanted to avoid the appearance of eagerness, to keep his bargaining power intact. So they indulged in some verbal sparring.

Lynch began with a bit of flattery. "I understand you know more about the motion-picture theatres in Detroit than anyone else. Is that true?"

George laughed. "Who is your informer?"

"Have you ever thought about coming back in the business?"

"Not very seriously, I think."

Lynch feinted with, "We are playing with the idea of new management in Detroit."

"Is that so?" George remembered that at the time of the sale, one of the verbal agreements was that no key personnel be changed. George felt that he had built up an organization which functioned smoothly and profitably and that it would be a mistake to disturb a winning team. Within three days after the sale some of the personnel had been changed! The replacements did not do so well, and with this added to the general poor business conditions, the situation was bad.

Lynch went on, "I have a couple of appointments this afternoon."

Trendle refused the bait and remained silent. He would like that job! He felt he needed the extra income until the radio station, which was simply not producing the profit he had hoped for, recovered. This would be it! But he realized that his bargaining power would be cut considerably if he appeared anxious. He remained silent.

Lynch went on, "I would prefer to have you, Mr. Trendle—that is, if you would like the job—but I must have your answer. Tomorrow morning in court I must present a name with enough power to get immediate acceptance."

"That's not much notice."

"No; and I'm going to New York, by train, at seven o'clock."

Trendle saw this as an opportunity to gain more bargaining time. "Isn't that a coincidence? It happens that I'm going to New York tonight too!"

George, who had had no previous thought of going to New York at that time, made his reservation. The men met on the train that night, and the deal was worked out before they retired.

The deal: George was to have a free hand with management and personnel. He would have about $50,000 a year as a salary, plus a percentage of the profit. He immediately, on his return from New York, began to reassemble his team of workers.

If George regretted his retreat from the plan to enter politics, he didn't have time to dwell on it. With the theatres and the radio station, he had considerable work, but he loved work and he was happy.

XIX

"I COULDN'T HAVE COME BACK to the theatres at a worse time," Trendle was thinking as he went through the reports on his desk. The year he had sold the theatres the profit was over $900,000. The year after the sale, under different management, the operation showed a deficit. His new contract read that he must return the theatres to a profitable operation. This stipulation was tough in view of business conditions, but Trendle never doubted that he could do it.

His first step was to return the theatres to their former format. Changing the type had confused patrons, who began to go to other theatres. Certain theatres had carried certain types of programs. Patrons knew what to expect from each theatre. The Michigan was designated as family-type entertainment and never deviated from that plan. This was for motion pictures. Where vaudeville-carrying programs were concerned, another factor entered the picture.

The stock-market crash had put many of the vaudeville artists, even the better-known ones, in great financial distress. Bookings were possible at more reasonable prices now.

The movie makers and exhibitors were hit hard by the depression. Bankruptcy and receivership held Paramount-Publix, RKO and the western divison of Fox. Bankers held these mortgages, and being bankers, were shrewd enough to want management of the theatres turned back to the men with the know-how, the former owners. They were right.

In Detroit the theatres came back into the black. Unhampered by partners, and given a free hand by the owners, Trendle was having a great time. He visited the theatres personally, and he watched the acts as well as the books. Most of all, he watched audience reaction. There were many incidents which stayed in his memory long after he retired from the theatres. One of these follows:

To please a largely feminine audience, he had booked a popular-style show, wherein the lead was a vivacious, good-looking young woman with a figure which outshone those of her models. She was thoroughly imbued with show business. Trendle, meaning to be agreeable only, complimented the girl highly. When a note came from her asking him to drop in at her dressing room, he went without hesitation.

He knocked at her door. It was opened and he stepped into a most enthusiastic welcome. The girl flung both arms around him, knocking off his glasses. They fell to the floor, broken. Realizing how taken aback the man was, she apologized. Trendle accepted her apology. Later she wrote to him from Battle Creek, where she was playing, and the letter began: "Dear Mr. Trendle: I am so sorry about the glasses, very, very sorry, and to show you just how sorry, if you were here, I'd kiss you on your dear bald head."

The episode had no importance for Trendle and would have been forgotten immediately except for one thing. He was puzzled, not at the letter, nor at the second apology, but at the behavior of his secretary. The mail, as usual, was opened and sorted by her. This letter was carefully placed at the top of the other mail. While she mentioned every other letter in the pile, she ignored the top one and never did say a word about it. Neither did he, but he often wondered how she interpreted the letter.

Just as he had done in the former theatre days, Trendle was going back and forth to Hollywood. Often he took his wife with him. She met many of the Hollywood luminaries. The bright lights, the so-called glamour stars, did not impress her, but she did find some of them "interesting." W. C. Fields was very amusing, even to repeating an old act for her. Sometimes he recounted parts of old pictures as if they were a real part of his life. Mrs. Trendle was very amused.

She met Mae West, who made a special effort to convince her that though she portrayed sex and gay living on the screen, her real life bordered on the ascetic. True, she neither smoked nor drank.

All of this was fun for the Trendles, but the travel came to an abrupt end when George realized that the radio station was not producing the profit he had anticipated.

His contract with the theatre owner had a full year to run, but now that the theatres were on a paying basis, and it would be possible to hire someone who would demand less salary, the owners were willing to accept Trendle's resignation. At last his theatre days were over!

The Detroit *Times* read, "Second Act Curtain for Trendle. George W. Trendle, who, thirty-one years ago, opened Detroit's first motion picture theatre has today resigned and ended his association with the city's movie industry."

The Detroit *Free Press* wrote, "The resignation of George W. Trendle is a matter of real regret"; and the Detroit *News,* listing his various activities, said he had "made such a conspicuous success of the theatre business and knows the likes and dislikes of the entertainment loving public and he will find new problems in radio." The article ended on a laudatory note for his contribution to the city.

But Trendle left the theatres with little or no regret. He had done a good job, and he knew it. Now he was looking forward to increasing the earnings of the radio station. With the enthusiastic help of his organization, he would build, build, build, until this station was up there with the best of them. His theme was, "Better shows make more patrons and bring more sponsors, and more sponsors bring more revenue."

He heard of a conflict between two radio stations in

Grand Rapids, Michigan. He bought both and combined them into WOOD, the first step in forming the Michigan Radio Network. "Good," thought he. "Now to make it all pay off."

"George," said King, "I think this is a losing fight."

"We're hardly in the ring, Mr. King. The real fight starts now."

King chuckled. He had utmost faith in George, but occasionally he faltered in that faith; he needed reassurance.

Herbert Hoover, then Secretary of Commerce, was explaining the new commission appointed by the President, the Federal Communications Commission, to police radio stations. "The ether is a public medium and its use must be for public benefit," said Hoover.

As George read the article he fingered a stack of unpaid bills. "I wonder if they'd like to pay these," he thought ruefully. So far much of the running expense had come out of the pockets of King and Trendle. It was a sad fact that the station was little more than self-supporting as it was managed now.

It was giving the public something for nothing. The public loved it. Owning a set involved no tax, no danger of political involvement, and most of all, no charge for the finest entertainment. If the public realized that the payment came from the small increase in price of the advertised goods, it was a mere passing thought.

When the station was bought, it had a network affiliation —the Columbia Broadcasting Company. Networks furnish talent to local stations in return for time to advertise their own sponsored products. Shortly after the acquisition of the station it was decided by the new owners that the affiliation was not so profitable as it could be, and so the contract was dropped and station WXYZ went independent

The former owners naturally had presented a rosy picture of the station's profit-making potential. And the new owners recognized this as a selling technique. They knew it was up to them to make the station pay.

The inherited personnel was not proving satisfactory. Looking around for replacements, George interviewed a young man who had been contacting downtown merchants and doing well at selling advertising for the Detroit *Journal.*

It was said of George Trendle, "He has a genius for choosing the right person for the right job. He does not make many mistakes at this." This was true, and it was proved over and over by the caliber of the men he hired, by their accomplishments in their jobs and by the length of time the men stayed with the organization. The new young man was H. Allen Campbell, later to become one of the best-known men in the business. Of him Trendle said, "I think Allen Campbell is one of the finest salesmen in the country. His salesmanship was a big factor in making WXYZ a dominant station in Detroit." As the station grew Trendle had many reasons to congratulate himself on his choice. Campbell was sales manager, later a stockholder, and in another project a partner–and always a good friend.

"Things are picking up," George told King.

"Good, George. Do you know how much this venture is costing me?"

"I know–I'm paying an equal amount out of my pocket. I figure it has cost us about one hundred and fifty thousand dollars each."

"Well, George?"

"We'll get it back. We haven't forgotten how to produce entertainment."

"You'll have to do it; I'm fresh out of ideas."

The station was indeed begining to grow and to show a profit, when a major national disaster took the wind out of their sails. It was called Bank Holiday.

The banks were in trouble, and Governor Comstock of Michigan, thinking that all the banks needed was time, ordered a one-week bank holiday, during which breather the banks could straighten their affairs and find some remedy for their financial illness.

This was on a Sunday–February 13, 1933–when banks were ordinarily closed. No warning was given, and no individual or business could prepare for the money drought. With few exceptions, within a week all of the banks in the nation were closed. No one had any money!

"How are you fixed for money, Mr. King?" George asked.

"If you mean cash, George, I have very little. How about you?"

"I just cashed a small personal check for my own running expense, but I don't have any large amount of cash."

"What about payroll for the station?"

The new station owners found themselves with a rapidly growing business and with no money to pay employees or material bills or even utilities. In order to survive, a way had to be found to house, clothe and feed the station personnel. It was a desperate situation. The fact that it was shared by thousands of organizations from coast to coast did not solve any problem for the owners of WXYZ. Utility bills and material bills could be had on credit, but the employees' living expense had to be met.

Allen Campbell justified the faith that George had in him. With his usual skill as an entrepreneur he went to the Fort Shelby Hotel and asked for credit for the station employes, and he got it. The entire crew and their dependents were housed and fed at the hotel for the duration of the bank holiday. Except, of course, King and Trendle, who lived in their own homes–Trendle at the Hotel Whittier and King dividing his time between northern Michigan and Detroit.

Meeting after meeting of the managing personnel met to

discuss the path the station should take. George had managed a good contract with the American Broadcasting Company when it was decided that the earlier going independent was an error. But George felt, and the others agreed, that the ability to produce good theatre shows should not be lost and that it would be well for WXYZ to produce some of its own radio shows locally.

What happened next had such spectacular results as to make history in the field of radio. No one who was born before the thirties or even during them can forget the flurry of excitement that followed the evening meal in most of the homes in America.

Radio, during the day, was, *Variety* said, "lugubrious and the pace torpid." If you had listened to NBC, for instance, from 10:15 A.M. to 6 P.M., you would have slid from one soap opera into another, with interruptions for commercials only. Except for commercials, there was a solid eight-hour period of one problem after another, beginning with "Lara Lawton" and ending with "Front Page Farrell."

There were reasons for this procession: the authors of the serials were not the highest paid and the stars not well known. The cost was small compared with that of other forms of entertainment and hence profitable to the producer. Moreover, the public did not complain–at least, not much.

This was the time of the Depression. The little housewife, on her knees scrubbing the floor, listened as she worked. The unpaid grocer, the milkman, even the utility company, faded into the background. Compared with the problems of the radio heroine, the little housewife's problems were small. For her, "life was just a bowl of cherries." If a tear dropped into the scrub bucket, it was because she, knowing trouble, could identify with the heroine. And identifying, she accepted with few restrictions the whole of the ballyhoo at the end of the program. The programs were pure corn, but no one has ever proved that corn does not sell products!

One of these programs ran around the noon hour, when George ordinarily was on his way to his office. He usually turned his radio on, and before long he was a regular listener. He listened and analyzed and analyzed and analyzed.

Perhaps he remembered the stanza from one of James Russell Lowell's poems:

When I was a beggarly boy,
And lived in a cellar damp,
I had not a friend nor a toy,
But I had Aladdin's lamp.

Never a beggarly boy and never living in anything but a good middle-class home as a boy, he nevertheless gained much inspiration from the books he had read. He had read everything he could lay his hands on from the moment he learned enough English to understand what he read. These were his lamp–James Fenimore Cooper, military-hero producer; Nick Carter, whose mysteries were so enthralling; but most of all, Horatio Alger.

The format for the Alger books, the same for each of them, was a fatherless boy who rose from rags to riches through his industrious effort. Euphonious titles, one after the other, told little of the story: *Bound to Rise; Sink or Swim; Luck and Pluck; Go West, Young Man, Go West;* and ninety-six others, all with the same or similar plot. The standard pattern was first a minor success, and then, through a stroke of fate, the benefactor steps in and furnishes the financial aid on which the hero builds a fabulous fortune. Improbable? Many a young man had achieved outstanding success on this same premise.

Western stories by the score, by George Monroe, Zane Grey, J.F.C. Adams, embodied the hero as one line of a Bobby Dylan poem, "You're all of the country wrapped up in one man."

"This we can produce on radio–that one man!" thought Trendle. "That one man would be a symbol of justice, a righter of wrongs. He could be masked–working without personal profit."

He called a meeting of station personnel, anyone who could contribute an idea–a writers' conference. Such a conference is held early in the morning usually; ideas are sent drifting about in a hazy manner until someone pins them down. In the final analysis one person makes the decision to accept or reject, and that person was George Trendle–Trendle, with his gift of discerning what the public wants, what the public will accept, what will influence the public and what will not.

At such a meeting Trendle laid out his basic concept and asked how it sounded to them. The idea met with enthusiastic response. There followed many questions.

XX

"THIS GUY IS SO PERFECT as to be unbelievable," said one of the men present.

"It's our job to keep the perfection and make him believable!" Trendle replied. He was determined that his new western hero should remain with qualities which the younger generation would follow. Psychological weaknesses would only confuse them. Therefore a character had to be built which would first interest, then inspire.

"Would he be married, with a family of teen-agers?"

"No, he could not be married. Home responsibilties would tend to restrict him. Moreover, every teen-ager has his own ideas of family. No, no family. He has to be single.

"This program is aimed at youngsters. First, we want to do some real good with this program, and second, it has to pay its way. Youngsters are a big factor in choosing household products from radio commercials. And we aim to sell this program to a sponsor just as soon as it is made salable."

There were more questions. "He'll have to earn a living somehow. What will his profession be?"

"If this is to be a western, could this hero be a cowboy or a ranch owner?"

Trendle shook his head. "No, that wouldn't do either. Problems which the hero would solve would have a personal interest in them. This hero is totally unselfish."

"But he has to earn a living some way."

There was talk of a silver standard in the newspapers, and many financiers thought it might be possible. This could have been in the subconscious of the next speaker.

"Let him own a silver mine. Let him take just enough for running expense."

"Good!"

Trendle knew what he wanted. The hero would be a law enforcer. Later that was changed to an ex-lawman, so that if he had to work on the fringe of the law, he would have freedom to do what was needed.

"Why? What motivation would he have? Because some has to be provided to make the character plausible."

"Possibly an injury done to a member of his family or one of his neighbors by a band of thieving bandits." Trendle was sure of what he wanted, so sure that he went on, "He'd be one of a group of rangers–nine of them; all the others would have been killed by the bandits. This ranger would be left for dead! Rescued by an Indian, he swore, when he became well again, 'I'll devote the rest of my life to tracking down bandits.' He'd ride alone," said Trendle.

"The Lone Ranger," the group called in unison. "That's it!"

"He could wear a mask," Trendle went on.

"He'd have a silver mine and take just enough to cover his living expenses–"

Howard Pierce was tossing an aluminized penny into the air. "He could shoot silver bullets," said he.

"Ride a white horse."

"And the horse would be shod with silver."

The sun caught the glint of the coin Howard was tossing. "And the horse would be named Silver."

Thus was the hero born–a character so perfect as to be unbelievable but made plausible through a series of omissions and commissions. Here was one who would never deviate from the path of right. Here was one never burdened by the details of mundane living. Here was one who righted wrongs wherever they might be. And accepted no thanks, no gratitude, satisfied with the knowledge of a job well done. When the question came "Who was that man?" he would ride away.

Now the show needed the breath of life, and to give it that, writers were needed. Not just writers who were adequate —the firm already had those—but a writer who would take this hero to heart, live with him, dream with him and above all, make him real.

A young man from Buffalo, New York, had submitted a radio series, "Warner Lester—Manhunter," which Trendle had liked and bought for WXYZ. He telephoned the writer, outlining his idea for a new western. Would he be interested?

Fran Striker was very interested! Here was the hero, a large athletic man on a great white stallion, shod with silver shoes. His guns would be ivory-handled, and he would shoot silver bullets. He would be masked to preserve anonymity!

"No killing—and no violence except as it is necessary to the story," said Trendle.

"He could shoot to disarm his opponent—he could shoot to render him helpless." Fran fell right into the pattern, and he worked and worked and worked!

So did George Trendle. He read every single script, adding and deleting. More than fifteen revisions of the original script were made before he felt it was ready for a tryout. He carried his black briefcase home, and night after night he went over the script that was submitted that day. On his bedside stand were pencil and scratch pad, so that any idea he had after retiring would not be lost. No detail was left to chance.

Fran Striker worked, running all eight copies through his typewriter at once. To make it easier, thinking Fran might dictate the story, Trendle hired a secretary for him. Later someone said, "The only thing the secretary did was to place the carbons in the paper and ready them for Fran. As fast as she could arrange the papers, Fran typed."

Finally, George decided his brainchild was ready. The tryouts were late at night; it was a fifteen-minute program, but it was soon seen that in order to tell a good, coherent story, it had to be lengthened. And so it became a thirty-minute show.

The call to the horse was rehearsed over and over again, and still George was not satisfied. So out at the station the employees there began to call to each other, in an effort to find a suitable call. "Hi-Yi, come on," "Yippee, let's go" . . . until one day someone called, and no one can remember who, "Hi Yo Silver, Away."

"That's it–that's just right–it has vibrancy, it's short–it rings!"

George Trendle watched over this, his own baby, with an eagle eye. Having achieved his dream of giving something to the youth of America, an ideal, he was going to make sure that nothing marred the ideal. For instance, the Lone Ranger didn't smoke, or drink, or swear, or use slang. Violence necessary to the story was never emphasized out of proportion.

There existed between Striker and Trendle a kind of *mitgefühl.* In German this implies sympathy and understanding but a little more of each than English implies.

Now it was decided that in the story someone would have to ferret out the wrongdoers for the Ranger to go after! The story needed a companion for the Ranger, someone to whom he could talk, developing the story. Since romance had been ruled out of the hero's life, it couldn't be a woman. It had to be someone as free as the Ranger himself–someone who wouldn't detract from the glory of the Ranger, someone who would talk little, contribute much, even a rescue if necessary.

At last the companion was perfected. It would be an Indian, the Indian who had found the Lone Ranger and nursed him back to health after the bandits had left him for dead.

And the Ranger called him "Tonto, faithful companion, trusty scout, Ke-mo Sah-be."

XXI

Music—The William Tell Overture

Sound effects—hoofbeats

Announcer—"From out of the past come the thundering hoofbeats of the Great Horse Silver—THE LONE RANGER RIDES AGAIN."

WHEN THIS STIRRING INTRODUCTION came out of the dome-shaped box, much of America was listening. When for the next half hour the Lone Ranger rode, between seven-thirty and eight o'clock, millions of listeners rode with him! For here was a man they wished they were or could be, honest, sincere, adventuresome. Here was a man with whom everyone would like to identify. Youngsters dreamed of themselves in the saddle, galloping across the plains, righting wrongs, making a pathway to justice and glory. For them every last detail was drunk in, soon to be emulated in their play and plans. Oldsters rode too, vicariously enjoying the action, the idealism, the certain good end that "right prevails always."

Now, the owner of this show felt he needed to test the audience. He needed to know if it was as powerful as he felt it was. And so an offer was made on the show to send a popgun to every child who wrote in and asked for it. The offer was made on a Tuesday night. The response was so great that even George had trouble believing it. The offer said that the first three hundred who wrote in qualified for the gift. On Thursday the Lone Ranger announced that the supply of popguns was exhausted. On Saturday he asked the audience not to write in.

The offer had brought a record response of 24,909 letters,

and this was from a station which barely reached outside the state of Michigan, from a program broadcast late at night.

The Detroit post office told Trendle that this volume was exceeded only by the number received by Father Coughlin who had at the time a coast-to-coast hookup.

George, though amazed at the response, wanted still another test. On Belle Isle, the island park in the Detroit River, every summer the Department of Parks and Recreation of the City of Detroit put up circus seats for three or four thousand people. A small circus was provided for the kids. It was an afternoon planned for the young people. Howard O. Pierce had made arrangements with the commission to have the Lone Ranger appear at intermission in between halves of the show on his white horse, make an appeal for safety, for respect for law and order and so forth. He would enter the ring, dismount and make his speech. Then he was to circle the ring a few times before he disappeared into the police truck which had brought him to the place.

The plan went as scheduled. The Ranger entered the ring. The white horse reared upward, then cantered around the ring. The Ranger dismounted and gave his talk–all exactly as planned except that as he left the ring the youngsters left behind him, following him until the police stepped in to allow the Ranger to get away.

The Department of Recreation, with a full-day planned program, lost their audience to the Ranger. They were not happy. But the staff at WXYZ, and particularly George Trendle, were delighted. Here was real proof of the popularity of the program. Campbell was eager to sell the program; he was successful at once. The Gordon Baking Company bought the program to advertise their Silver Cup Bread. The similarity of names was a coincidence. The first sponsored program went on the air November 27, 1933.

A month later the program was extended to WGN, Chicago; the next month it went to WOR, Newark. WGN, WXYZ and WOR then formed the Mutual Broadcasting Company, but WXYZ had very little authority since it was a 1,000-watt station and the other two had 50,000 watts.

Who acted the first Lone Ranger? A man named Deeds played six performances, and the title role was then turned over to George Stenius, who played it for a while. But Trendle continued to test "voices." He knew what he wanted, and he intended to test until he found a voice that was deep, vibrant, commanding, with authority–a voice that carried the connotation of all that the Lone Ranger stood for. He found it in Earl W. Grazer.

For six years, until his death in an automobile accident, Grazer was the Lone Ranger. Now he was gone, and the problem was to find a replacement who would keep the young audience. Audiences do not take kindly to replacements, and the program might suffer irreparable harm if one were attempted suddenly.

So Trendle told the writers to give the Lone Ranger an injury to his voice caused by a villain. For a couple of weeks he didn't speak at all; then he spoke for a couple of weeks in a whisper, during which time Tonto carried the show. Finally he was written in completely well and spoke in the voice the public came to know so well. That voice was Brace Beamer's; Brace stayed with the program the entire period that it remained on the air, as such. Beamer sounded like the Ranger, and he looked the part–a large man with splendid physique, athletic and a fine horseman. The success of the program was fantastic! The audience did its own advertising. If a milkman's horse started unexpectedly and broke into a trot, some kid was sure to holler, "Hi Yo Silver."

During World War II the Army used quotes from the Ranger shows as passwords. At a race track a horse who broke from the crowd and ran part of the distance was hailed "Hi

Yo Silver." A couple of debutantes from Chicago attended a fox hunt in England. The host of the young ladies asked, "What is that jolly cry you Yanks use to start a horse?" In unison the girls shouted, "Hi Yo Silver, Away!"

The musical introduction–the William Tell Overture–was the best-known of all classics to the general listening public. In Detroit it was decided to entertain and educate the children in music by having afternoon matinees of symphony music. Gabrilowitsch was conducting. Too busy playing music to listen to radio, Gabrilowitsch was unfamiliar with "The Lone Ranger" program and was utterly shocked when at the beginning, with the first few bars of the overture, enthusiastic members of his youthful audience shouted, "Hi Yo Silver!"

Mrs. Eleanor Roosevelt wrote in her newspaper column that her grandson Buzz preferred "The Lone Ranger" to her own bedtime stories. The audiences were not confined to children by any means. Letters poured into the station–many of them from shut-ins who lived adventurous lives vicariously through the Ranger.

The appeal was so great that magazines picked up the idea and wrote stories about the Lone Ranger and advertised the show themselves with the free publicity.

In October of 1936 the Lone Ranger told the children to go to the neighborhood grocer, get a safety pledge card and send it to the station, which would send them a Lone Ranger badge as evidence of their pledge. The pledge was a written promise to tell the truth at all times, be helpful when possible, never to cross streets except at crossings–and exercising care then–not to play in the streets, and more. The first six weeks after the offer almost five thousand badges were distributed. Millions of masks and photographs of the Lone Ranger were sent out.

Fran Striker had done his research well, but he had never been west of the Mississippi, and sometimes an error crept in.

George Trendle watched for these, and they rarely escaped him. If one did, letters poured into the station (giving further evidence of the power of the program), but sometimes the audience was so caught up in the interest of the story that a flagrant mistake went by without a comment. The radio station's offices were on the seventeenth and eighteenth floors of the Stroh Building (later called the Mutual Building), but the broadcasting studio was at first atop the Maccabbees Building, and later out on Jefferson Avenue. Air conditioning was not general, and windows were opened for air and comfort.

The life of the Lone Ranger was placed in the late 1800's, yet in the middle of one of the programs an automobile horn was heard. So caught up in interest was the audience that not a single letter of protest came in.

Charles Livingstone, a young actor with the Jessie Bonstelle players, came into the picture as director of the Ranger shows. He watched like a hawk for just such errors—he watched for situations which might lead the young people into misinterpreting a situation. He knew the Boss's feeling about the program—it had to be something of an inspiration to the youth—and he judged its merits by the reaction of his own two children. It was written in one of the scripts that in order to flush the villain out, a fire was built in the bushes near the house. "Whoops!" said Charles.

"What's wrong?" asked Striker

Livingtone replied, "Kids might get the idea that it would be fun to light fires to flush out their playmates."

"What kid would think that?" asked Striker.

"Mine would," said Livingstone.

The scene was rewritten willingly by Striker on the spot.

Fran Striker took his hero, the Lone Ranger, very seriously—probably almost as seriously as did George Trendle, who created the hero; and Chuck Livingstone involved himself so thoroughly that he patterned a child's behavior by the example left by the Long Ranger. And the Lone Ranger continued to draw larger and larger audiences.

When, during the latter part of 1937, someone in the management at Gordon Baking Company felt they had exhausted the advertising value of the Lone Ranger to their product, Allen Campbell went to New York and immediately sold the program to Bond Bread.

At first the shows were live–that is, they went out on the air as they were acted out in the studio. But later, in February of 1938, the shows were offered in transcription form. And "The Lone Ranger" was heard over 140 radio stations, including Newfoundland, Ontario, New Zealand and Hawaii. In America three shows weekly met a receptive public.

The profit was greater than that of any other show on the air. This creation, by one man for the purpose of educating the young to greater moral values, was paying off handsomely. Fantastic as the show was, the proceeds realized from the sale of products bearing the name "The Lone Ranger" were equally fantastic.

Republic Studios were licensed to make two full-length motion pictures for theatre distribution, subject to restrictions. There was a cartoon strip for King Theatres, the William R. Hearst Corporation color-features department. Novelties tied to the program were sold–pins, rings, badges, boots, outfits and a dozen other items with the name "The Lone Ranger" attached.

The success of "The Lone Ranger" was bound to bring people who claimed to be its originator. The legal department, in every case, convinced the courts that George W. Trendle was the sole creator. Fran Striker was once mentioned as the originator perhaps because he was permitted to write several books "based on the adventures of the Lone Ranger, created by George W. Trendle." All carried this notation. One such book was sent to Trendle, *The Silver Bullet,* dated December

25, 1951, and autographed by Fran Striker in his own handwriting, "To George W. Trendle, from one who chronicles the saga of his brainchild." This book is among Trendle's prized mementos.

Occasionally some claimant would spring up, with no basis in fact. At times there was litigation. Raymond J. Meurer defended the Lone Ranger Corporation and always successfully.

Contracts for the sale of novelties and premiums were all drawn or handled by Meurer, of whom Trendle said, "Ray is a brilliant lawyer, and he handled these contracts during the entire life of the show." He went on, "When negotiating for the licensing of many of our shows for radio, television or motion pictures, we always had a three-cornered conference: H. Allen Campbell, who did the actual selling; Raymond J. Meurer, who handled the contracts; and I, who created the programs and took care of the administrative department of the corporation. Each of us handled his own department, and the combined results were very satisfactory."

The contracts, which were worked out for all the shows, were never broken. Ray, who had done the final legal work, stopped at least a dozen would-be imitators who wanted to hitch onto the glory of "The Lone Ranger" or any of the other shows.

Raymond J. Meurer began his career as a musician in the Michigan Theatre orchestra. Just as Trendle had done, Ray studied law at night school, was graduated and came into the organization to handle some of the legal work for radio station WXYZ. Eventually Ray became full-time legal representative, and it was made possible for him to acquire some stock.

He had still another talent–a particular knack for negotiating labor contracts. He went on and up in the organization and was placed in charge of the licensing of the sale of "gimmicks." In other words, after a contract was made with the Hearst organization for a comic strip, Ray began to license the sale of belts, hats, rings, and a myriad of other like articles. As they were introduced in this market a very good profit was realized from these too. Trendle said, "If, as one of my friends says, I have a genius for selecting the right man for the right job, these men certainly proved right for their jobs: Campbell, Meurer, Pierce, Striker and Livingstone. In each case I made a right choice, I am happy to say."

Trendle had built up a splendid organization. A writer once said of him, "He has a Euclidian mind." In any case he had found the formula to please the public; to teach, without seeming to teach, the lesson "Right must prevail." To do this "next to impossible task," a good well-rounded organization was essential.

"When the plot for 'The Lone Ranger' was devised," said George Trendle, "and we hired Fran to dramatize our ideas, he showed an extremely high degree of creativity–built up a staff of writers. He grasped the general idea of the hero–the Lone Ranger–and did an excellent job of carrying out the ideals. From selling scripts for five dollars each in Buffalo, he grew to be one of the highest-paid writers in the business," and, Trendle continued with emphasis, "he was worth every penny." Again, "We tried other writers at first, but the scripts that Fran turned out or supervised were always the best.

"Charles Livingstone worked at first as an announcer, and occasionally as an actor, but when we went into producing, he asked for a chance to direct. At once his ability was evident. He was great! Eventually he needed an assistant, and Fred Flowerday came to us."

The Ranger stayed on the air three times a week until television, and over 3,000 radio shows were made.

XXII

"THE GREEN HORNET" opening:

Sound effect: Buzzz

Announcer: THE GREEN HORNET

Music: Timpani roll

Announcer: He hunts the biggest of all game. PUBLIC ENEMIES WHO TRY TO DESTROY OUR AMERICA!

Music: Theme: (Flight of the Bumblebee)

Announcer: WITH HIS FAITHFUL VALET, KATO, BRITT REID, DARING YOUNG PUBLISHER, MATCHES WITS WITH THE UNDERWORLD, RISKING HIS LIFE THAT CRIMINALS AND RACKETEERS, WITHIN THE LAW, MAY FEEL ITS WEIGHT BY THE STING OF THE GREEN HORNET.

Sound effect: Black Beauty (car takes off)

Announcer: RIDE WITH BRITT REID IN THE THRILLING ADVENTURE OF: . . .

"The Green Hornet" came into being some time during 1935 and was on the air for the first time on January 31, 1936. It was natural that once he had assembled so fine an organization, George would put it to its fullest use. When questioned, George would say that he believed that "The Green Hornet" was the best of all the shows he produced.

"It had mystery, it had melodrama, and yet it was believable. Every story was based on everyday items which appeared in any big-town newspaper."

Although "Thc Green Hornet" was aimed at a more adult

audience than "The Lone Ranger," the similarities were there. Both heroes remedied conditions beyond the reach of the law. Both were masked. If the "fiery horse with the speed of light" was missing, there entered a super-super automobile–the Black Beauty–which could outdistance any other automobile in the world.

The hero's helper and companion became Kato, the learned scientist, who used his skill during the day to invent devices, including the car, the gun which paralyzed but never killed and other items to further the cause. At night he rode beside the Green Hornet.

The Green Hornet was a modernization of the Lone Ranger, aimed at an older audience. Just as the Lone Ranger aimed at pleasing and influencing the youngsters, so the Green Hornet told the young voters, "This can happen in your town, and a crooked politician can succeed unless you, the voter, stop him."

The hero–the Hornet–was an educated man, and his English was not violated by slang or profanity. He was publisher of the *Daily Sentinel* by day, but by night he was a "racketbuster waging a fight to bring lawbreakers to justice"–the lawbreakers who operated within the legal edges but outside the moral sides of the law.

The Hornet stories were modern in their day; and there were, among the audience, people to whom the Hornet was so real that they wrote letters, "We have a crooked mayor down here–and we need the Green Hornet," or, "We suspect the members of our City Council are filling their own pockets. Can you send the Hornet down to clean up this mess?" Many believed the Hornet to be a real person with real powers to cope with criminals and near-criminals.

George Trendle said of it, " 'The Green Hornet' is as good today as ever because all of the ingredients of the story still exist: the crooked politician, the villain who operates within the law, the extortionist, the blackmailer who uses his knowledge to make someone else do his dirty work. All of these things exist; they do not, unfortunately, become outmoded. 'The Green Hornet' could still be an effective force for good. And it could be a very entertaining program."

J. Edgar Hoover, director of the Federal Bureau of Investigation, said, "The Green Hornet is a force for good."

XXIII

"What I'd really like," said Trendle, "is another show—one to bridge the gap between the Lone Ranger's audience of children and the Green Hornet's audience of young adults."

He discussed this with Striker, who agreed. "We could work up something entirely different, different background, different kind of character. Make it a new show entirely."

"No," said Trendle, "not too different. We now have a winning combination. Let's keep it that way."

Something from the old Rex Beach stories sprung up in his mind to prompt him to say, "The Yukon—it has always been a good background for adventure, and it is different from the shows we now have."

"The hero could still be a lawman," said Striker.

Trendle came back quickly, "A Northwest Mountie! We could build a good Canadian audience."

And so another show was born!

CHALLENGE OF THE YUKON

(Later changed to "Sergeant Preston of the Yukon")

Sound effects: Wind

Announcer: CHALLENGE OF THE YUKON

Preston: On, King: On, you Huskies

Sound effect: King and the dogs bark

Announcer: GOLD! GOLD IS DISCOVERED IN THE YUKON! BACK TO THE DAYS OF THE GOLD RUSH AND THE ADVENTURES OF SERGEANT PRESTON AND HIS WONDER DOG, YUKON KING, AS THEY MEET THE CHALLENGE OF THE YUKON IN THEIR RELENTLESS PURSUIT OF LAWBREAKERS.

Music Theme–Donna Diana Overture

Trendle achieved another dream–he had his own shows right across the board. On Monday, Wednesday and Friday, "The Lone Ranger" was heard; on Saturday, "The Green Hornet"; and on Tuesday and Thursday, "The Challenge of the Yukon"–all sponsored and all national, all at seven-thirty all week–the only case in history where one producer had the same time slot for the entire week with his own shows!

At first the whole story of "The Challenge of the Yukon" revolved around the dog–a husky named Yukon King. Yukon King, the story goes, was rescued by Sergeant Preston of the Northwest Mounted Police when the she-wolf who had kidnaped him from his own mother was attacked by a lynx. The Sergeant was able to drive off the lynx but not in time to save the mother. The Sergeant took the young puppy back to his barracks.

"I am going to call you King–Yukon King. I'll teach you to respect good men and to hate evil ones. Your instinct will show you the difference. You'll learn to captain a team of dogs and to pull your own weight as well. I'll teach you how to practice self-control and how best to use your great strength. We shall be partners. You'll be the greatest dog in all of the Yukon."

Such, in a nutshell, was the theory behind all the shows which Trendle monitored so carefully. It was the positive victory of right over evil; and the general public never tires of the theme. Everybody wants to be the good guy.

Later on the name was changed to "Sergeant Preston of the Yukon," again to simplify identification of the audience with the hero.

Sergeant Preston and King rode the snow country together, King, as he was later known, running "free lead" with the dog team, keeping the other dogs in order. The more recalcitrant he nipped; the others he nudged back into line, earning a pat on the head and a "Good dog, King" from his master. There were times when King rescued his master, because the Sergeant was not so quick as King to recognize the black heart of the crooked villain.

Three shows "straight across the board" and Trendle monitored every single one of them, and through Chuck Livingstone, hired and secured the highly talented people it took to play the shows. Thus he ensured their success.

With this many there were bound to be differences of opinion. These were brought before Trendle, and occasionally he would make a decision, but more often than not he would toss the question back and forth between the arguing parties and they would settle it themselves.

Mickey Merrill, now Mrs. Stephen Gross, wrote many of the Yukon scripts.

"There were many situations which later seemed humorous. We were like one big family, and we fought like one big family. I am sure we gave 'the chief' many a headache. We were all more or less odd-balls, and I get many a laugh recalling some of the incidents. Temperamental blowups were almost a daily occurrence." She went on, "Chuck Livingstone was directing Paul Sutton in a part on 'The Lone Ranger' show. Paul was a villain who was supposed to have been vanquished, one way or another, and die! At rehearsal Chuck said, 'I don't quite like the way you die—'

" 'Don't tell me how to die. I have died forty times in the movies and if anyone knows how to die, I do.'

"Chuck shouted back, 'You may know how to die in the movies, but you don't know one-two-three about dying on radio.' "

And so the show went on. "Sutton was an excellent actor—and Livingstone was a fine director."

With this organization, George looked around again for another show. "We had all the ingredients," he said.

XXIV

THE AMERICAN AGENT

Sound effects:

Music:

Announcer: The American Agent! He walks alone through jungles of intrigue! Around him hangs an air of mystery and the ominous threat of death. Unknown, accompanied only by Truth and Courage, moves Bob Barclay–American Agent!

ON THE SURFACE, IN THE STORY, the American Agent was a foreign correspondent working in foreign countries for an American newspaper but actually using his newspaper connections to observe and correct situations in foreign countries, as they affected America, without getting personally involved. He reported and set about to remedy whatever the situation demanded.

"I still have fifty-two records of the show 'The American Agent,' " said Trendle.

"Would this show be apropos to these times?"

"Indeed it would," replied Trendle. "We have real-life stories in the newspapers which prove these things can happen. This was, at the time of its broadcasting, a very popular show, and everyone was pleased with it. It went very well indeed, until 'American Arrested in Czechoslovakia as Spy,' the newspapers read one morning."

It was William Otis, who really was a foreign correspondent, not a spy. The secretary walked into Trendle's office and announced a Mr. So-and-So (his name long since lost in the files) from the United States Government. Always cooperative with the government, George rose to greet the man.

"What can I do for you?" he asked after the usual amenities.

"I am here about your show 'The American Agent.' "

"How do you like the show?"

"Very good—in fact, it's too good."

George laughed. "I don't know about that, but the Peter Paul Company, who sponsored it, thought it an excellent show, I am happy to say."

"In that way, no doubt, it is good too. But now we are having a lot of trouble about our foreign correspondents."

"What does that have to do with the show?"

"Well, as I said, the show is too good. In fact, it is so good that in many of the European countries it is thought to be taken from life. They think the stories are true stories, dramatized over here."

"Nonsense! It's just a good spy story—they've been going on since the Trojan horse or even before."

"Mr. Trendle, we can't force you to take the show off the air, but we are hoping you will think the situation over. Mr. Otis is still incarcerated in a Czechoslovakian prison."

"I'll think it over."

Trendle did think it over—and was still wondering if, in fact, the show could influence foreign governments or if it would be used as an excuse to jail our newspapermen, when he had another caller.

It was the president of the Association of Foreign Correspondents.

"Mr. Trendle, we can understand your position regarding this show."

George wasn't sure he understood that. He was very sincere in believing that the show had nothing to do with Otis' being in jail, so he said nothing.

The man went on, "We don't have the right to ask you to

discontinue the show, but we hope you will change its format. Perhaps your agent, the hero in the story, could work in America. Oh, I'm not telling you how to write your shows—but some change that would take the show out of Europe, at least until we can get Otis out of jail."

"I knew," said George recounting the experience, "that if I changed the format, it would overlap other shows of the spy type. I felt that changing the format changed the show and it would be better to take it off the air than to destroy its impact. At that time it was running opposite the 'Inner Sanctum' show, a darned good show, and 'The Agent' was topping it in ratings. Still, when a man's life may be at stake, anything one could do, even if there are doubts about its effectiveness, should be done. I took 'The American Agent' off the air. Otis was released some time later, and if I shortened his stay in prison as much as a day, I am glad to have done so."

Six months later Trendle was puzzled that a European-made show, sponsored by the Ford Company, called "Foreign Intrigue," was aired on a national network. Trendle saw a great similarity between the basic plot of "The American Agent" and "Foreign Intrigue." In his opinion, however, the show was badly written and poorly produced. It stayed on the air for five months and then went off, with no explanation.

XXV

NO EXPERIENCE IS COMPLETE in itself, they say. It either lives on in its own consequences or it creates new experience itself. This was brought home to George in a most peculiar way.

In addition to the radio station which he controlled, he kept interest in several other businesses. One of these a radio-repair shop. In the early days one of the difficulties of radio owners and radio broadcasters was keeping the sets and the senders in good working order.

George opened a radio-repair shop on Broadway, a few blocks from his own office. He hired a well-recommended mechanic and from then on took little part in the management of the shop.

"Mr. Trendle, I've got to see you at once." It was his manager's voice over the telephone.

"What's wrong?"

"I can't tell you over the phone. I've got to see you."

Arriving at the office, he told the following story:

It seemed he had been approached by what looked like a good business account. He was to keep some sending equipment in working order for a ham operator. In pursuit of the business, the manager said, he was called to an office on Michigan Avenue, across the street from the Book-Cadillac Hotel (now called the Sheraton-Cadillac). He was met at the downstairs door by two men, each of whom took one of his arms and escorted him up the stairs. This odd reception was made even more strange by the fact that the men let their hands stray over his hips and shoulders as if searching for hidden weapons. "Just like a gangster movie," the manager said.

At the top of the stairs one of the men heightened the similarity to the gangster picture by knocking three times, stopping and knocking twice more. A slot in the door opened. The door was opened, the men stepped aside, and he stood alone in the dimly lighted room. When his eyes became accustomed to the lack of light, he saw the room. It was beautifully furnished–a large room with a desk at one end of it.

Behind the desk a small dark-haired man said, "I got a little boat on the Detroit River."

"Yes?"

"We run it back and forth between here and Canada."

"Yes?"

"We pick up a little stuff over there."

The manager, taking care to appear unsurprised, nodded.

"Now," said the little man, "the problem is to know exactly when to do this–uh–picking up."

No response.

"So we made a plan; it's right up your alley. We have a little radio transmitter and we play music. Like when our man at the customs office down there sees the customs men are looking elsewhere, he telephones us and we play something like 'Barney Google with the googly-googly eyes.' If the government man gets back on the job, we play something like 'Yes, we have no bananas.' Now, that way our boat on the other side of the river knows when they can come over without interference. . . ." He hesitated. The radio-shop manager encouraged him by repeating, "Barney Google, eh?"

"Oh, we change the songs every time the telephone rings, almost."

"Pretty ingenious," said the manager.

"Oh, sure," the little man went on, "we got it all worked out–but we got one problem. That so-and-so transmitter keeps breaking down, and we haven't got a good man to fix it."

The manager nodded.

"We need a good man to keep it running. We can give you, say four hundred dollars a week. It wouldn't take you more than one hour a week and you could keep us going good."

"I'd have to talk it over with the owner of the shop."

"Sure–sure–you talk it over."

The manager gave the whole story to George, knowing he would veto the proposition unequivocally. George, of course, said no; he would not be interested in the least.

Returning to the Michigan Avenue address, the manager was taken up the stairs in the same manner: one man at each elbow, searching for hidden weapons–the signal knocks at the door–the little man behind the desk.

"We can't take on any extra business with anyone on a continuing basis," said the manager.

"You talked to your boss?"

"Yes; he made the decision."

"Then it's okay with me. Your boss is some king of a guy! He's not afraid of anyone! Years ago, I asked him a favor, and he did it. No ifs or buts about it–he did it. The police were dragging me in for no reason whatever, and I asked him to get in touch with somebody and have it stopped. He went to the Commissioner. The Commissioner investigated me–but good! And from then on, no bothering by cops!

"I just wanted to give him a chance to get in on a good thing–if he wanted to, that's all. You tell him for me it's okay."

It was the same "Joe Doakes" who had been recommended by Burt Brown in the old motion-picture days!

XXVI

"I WISH WE COULD RIDE a little nearer to home, George," remarked Mrs. Trendle as they left for their morning horseback ride.

It was 1933, when Trendle was married, sold the house on LaSalle Boulevard and took his bride to the Whittier, a large residential hotel on the shore of the Detroit River. They were awaiting the completion of their new house in Grosse Pointe Shores. Together they watched the construction of the beautiful house, while they planned the furnishings to the tiniest detail. Often they would drive out and hand in hand, along the shore of Lake St. Clair, walk as they discussed their new home.

Trendle's own family were settled into a good pattern. Young George was attending St. John's Military Academy in Wisconsin. His daughter Mary K. was in a private school in Cooperstown, New York. His older sister, Jen, had married Mark Kellogg, and his mother and sister Clara lived in an apartment nearby.

In business he had his three shows across the board six evenings a week. The radio station was doing well, too. The three "Lone Ranger" shows, the two Yukon shows and "The Green Hornet" were at the height of their popularity and brought in large revenue from his stockholdings. In addition, he was still managing the theatres at a sizable salary. Various investments were proving profitable as well. Income taxes were very low, and it was no time at all before he could forget the Depression. His affairs were in excellent condition.

He even had time for some recreation. He had continued his riding and at times considered other sports. He thought he might like to learn golf. And he tried. How he tried!

"Goodness knows I tried," said Trendle, "but golf was not for me."

He joined the Detroit Golf Club, took lessons there and felt he was not improving, so he left that club and joined the Bloomfield Hills Country Club. He took lessons, left after a little time, joined the Birmingham Country Club and took lessons again. Then he joined the Beechgrove Country Club in Canada, and more lessons. Finally he joined Lochmorr Country Club, and he seemed to be making some progress but felt he would never be a topnotch amateur golfer since golf required more time than he was willing to give it to reach expertise. So he gave up the whole idea of golf. In any case, having found riding as an exercise and sport, he was happy in it.

But from the Whittier in Detroit, where he and Mrs. Trendle waited for their home to be built, the distance to his riding club took more time than he wanted to give, and to comply with his wife's expressed wish, he began to investigate the club nearest their home, the Grosse Pointe Hunt Club. He was appalled to learn that it had been closed for some time.

"The club owes several thousand dollars, Mr. Trendle," said one of the members.

"Why don't the members get together and pay it?"

"It is possible that they can't or they won't–but either someone puts up the money or the club will be sold out or have to go into bankruptcy."

"Let me see what I can do." Here was a job tailor-made for Trendle's particular talent, raising money! He quickly found a dozen friends who would put up the required money, take over the management and reopen the club.

It would seem there had been quite a number of people waiting for just such a development. Membership picked up rapidly. But Trendle knew that no one belongs just for the sake of belonging and that some kind of inducement was needed, perhaps some unique entertainment. The Wednesday-night rides were resumed, but this time with an added little flair. Following the rides, a drawing was made and the prizes were tickets to the theatres which Trendle managed–small prizes, which any member could buy easily, but which had the added value of the thrill of winning. Membership continued to grow, and the club became financially responsible. Additional riding space was arranged with the Grosse Pointe Country Club, and the new bridle path was permitted along the edge of the golf course.

And Trendle was elected president of the club for four successive years, a job which he found too time-consuming. Further, the club was reopened, financially sound and growing, so the challenge for George was gone. A new president was elected.

Soon after the election the directors voted to borrow money from the National Bank of Detroit, pay off the investors and run the club themselves, a far simpler task now that the club was paying off. The original investors had charged no interest for the use of the money, but naturally the bank did charge interest.

In the meantime Grosse Pointe was growing at a rapid rate, and much of the property along the Hunt Club property was zoned as residential and was beginning to be subdivided. It began to appear that there would be little property for the riders from the Hunt Club. And George stepped in once more.

He made a firm offer on a piece of property adjacent to the Masonic Country Club and a five-year commitment with the club owners to use the space around the outer edge of the golf course for riding. Also, they agreed to allow the Hunt Club the use of locker rooms and of the dining room as well. The arrangement would have proved profitable for both clubs. The property sought consisted of thirty acres. The

Grosse Pointe Hunt Club House, which was on one corner of the property and covered three acres, could be sold for $25,000. So for a difference of $5,000 the Hunt Club would own this new property. Trendle envisioned selling the rest of the club property, riding rings, stables, etcetera, for enough to build a new riding ring indoors and a new outdoor riding ring and emerge with thirty or more acres of land. But the president and the directors were content to let well enough alone, and they turned down the proposition. However, Mr. and Mrs. Trendle continued to enjoy the riding and the fellowship of other members for many years.

Later on Trendle had another experience at rescuing clubs. Shortly after he moved into his new home on the shore of Lake St. Clair, the Grosse Pointe Yacht Club closed, owing the First National Bank of Detroit the sum of $128,000. This constituted a downright challenge to Trendle. Three or four other men who felt the same challenge urged him to attend a meeting at the Detroit club to see what could be done to save it.

On investigation it was learned that the National Bank, to rescue their original investment, would be willing to carry the mortgage further if they had a substantial payment on it, say $25,000. Another $25,000 would be needed to get the club started again. It was, therefore, a question of raising $50,000 at once.

Life memberships at $1,000 each were suggested. These would be dues-free and assessment-free–a real bargain for anyone wanting membership in this fine club. Fifty of these would put the club back in business. A tentative membership agreement was drawn up which the group immediately accepted. With these clauses–free membership for twenty-five years and no assessment, also the privilege of selling, if a member chose, the unexpired portion of the membership–the club memberships were actively sought. Trendle took three of them–one each for himself, his son and his son-in-law. He sold one to Allen Campbell. The other forty-six memberships sold in less than two weeks!

The Grosse Pointe Yacht Club House has been called the most beautiful clubhouse in America, and it is one of the outstanding yacht clubs in America. The club is located on Lake St. Clair, about half a mile east of Trendle's home. As he looks across at it from his windows it gives him a good deal of satisfaction to know that he had a large part in saving this fine club for the community.

XXVII

So came the thirties. The roaring twenties had come to a whining close! And the thirties arrived to take over the job of rehabilitation in the financial field. Other events of the thirties: The Japanese invaded Manchuria in 1931, Mussolini invaded Ethopia in 1935, and Hitler entered the Rhineland in 1936—all of which America disapproved but without giving any indication of a feeling of compulsion to interfere. So far as the Japanese invasion was concerned, that was too far away for intimate concern. The Ethiopians had little in common with the predominantly white society of America. As for the Hitler invasion, there were many people who preferred Germany to England. America preferred to sit between the oceans on an island of isolation.

History records that by 1937 both Hitler and Mussolini were involved in the Spanish civil war. The Japanese attacked China the following year. Austria, Czechoslovakia and the Low Countries were overrun with Hitler's forces. America stepped up its aid to the Allies, but not under that name.

The youth of America, who had until now protested that this European fracas was not of our making nor of our concern, began to feel the tie of common language. Some of them joined the Canadian army, some the English; a few went to Spain. The security of two oceans, the Atlantic and the Pacific, was being shaken. People reacted. They took sides in the foreign arguments and supported their arguments with words and work. In the evening they turned to radio for entertainment and for escape from reality.

And radio was peculiarly fitted to fill both roles. The stories were there, and the settings were simply sketched-in word pictures, leaving the listener to fill in the detail with his own imagination. Trendle provided straight across the board, at seven-thirty each night, an adventuresome swing through "righteousness land."

Audiences grew and grew. Trendle worked harder and harder to give his audiences that good "something for nothing" that would entertain and inspire. No one could know how many young lives were touched and affected by Trendle's brain children. He could only guess by the ratings and by the mail. To say that he was satisfied was an understatement; he was elated at the success of the shows.

How lucky he was! he told himself. How many men could supply inspiration which could outstrip even the Horatio Alger stories? And how many men could become wealthy in the process?

"What's wrong with that radio?" he called out, annoyed at its blaring volume.

His wife, who habitually rose earlier than her husband, came into view. "Oh, George, listen to it!"

It was December 7, 1941. Japan had fired on Pearl Harbor. Like it or not, we were now at war. Public-service time would have to be stretched. Every program which might touch on information useful to the enemy was either canceled or altered. Overnight wartime censorship was one thing, and another was the necessity to make room for services to the armed forces.

A citation reading, "For distinguished service rendered in behalf of the National War Savings program" was signed by Henry Morganthau, secretary of the United States Treasury, and presented to George W. Trendle.

A message from the Chairman of Radio to the State Council of Defense read, "Know ye that reposing special trust and confidence in the integrity and ability of George W. Trendle . . ." and was signed by Murray D. Von Wagoner, governor of Michigan.

These were war services which were rendered personally. What the station did to further our cause is in the records.

The record public service for Trendle was twenty-three years as a commissioner on the Board of Fire Commissioners. Three other men served with him for most of that time. They were Nate Shapiro, president of the Cunningham Drug Company; Arthur Winter, president of the Winter-Hebb Printing Company; and M. C. McMahon, superintendent of the Detroit Branch of American Car and Foundry Company. Two previous companions on the board had been Charles Clippert of the Clippert Brick Company and Gus Schantz, president of the Detroit Cleveland Navigation Company. In the twenty-three years Trendle had served under six different mayors, and each four years he took his place as president of the board.

The commission met each Monday afternoon to decide routine matters of policy. Firemen appeared before the board for major or minor infractions of rules, and punishment was meted out. Just as often the task was much more pleasant—praise for an act above and beyond the call of duty. During Trendle's terms there were many changes in policy, salaries and fringe benefits. General working conditions were improved.

Fire headquarters at the corner of Larned and Shelby streets was built and furnished with all the latest equipment. A large plaque listing the names of the commissioners at the time and headed by the president, George W. Trendle, is fastened to the wall on the building.

The commission had been formed years earlier to take the fire department entirely out of politics, and it operated as a separate entity through various elections of mayors. But at the end of twenty-three years the new mayor began to try to dictate policy, insisting on choosing the commission's secretary. The commission objected, and Trendle called on Mayor Van Antwerp, protesting this interference. The board had always been an independent body, apart from politics, and the commissioners felt they could not accept the mayor's policy-making plan. They had agreed that in order to bring this matter before the public if the mayor would not allow them to work without interference, they would resign in a body. All four men agreed.

While he was in California on business, Trendle received a letter from Mayor Van Antwerp requesting his resignation. As agreed, Nate Shapiro and Arthur Winter resigned with him. McMahon stayed on.

During his tenure as president Trendle appointed Dr. Carl Schulte as physician for the Fire Department. There began a friendship between the two men which has lasted through the years.

The next appointment was given him by Governor Harry F. Kelly, governor of the state of Michigan. He was made a member of the Board of Commissioners of the Huron-Clinton Metropolitan Authority. He served for sixteen years on this board, through four different governors, four times as president of the board. The commission covered five counties: Wayne, Macomb, Washtenaw, Huron and Oakland. During his service the five counties each passed resolutions, granting the commission one-half mill of their taxes, which money made it possible to build the various parks. The Huron Metropolitan Park, on the shore of Lake St. Clair in Macomb County, was made on what was originally a huge swamp. It was reclaimed with sand from the bottom of the lake. When completed, it had bathhouses, outdoor swimming pools, a dancing pavilion, picnic grounds, a golf course and a huge parking lot which could accommodate 7,500 cars. It is still altogether one of the most modern and complete recreational areas in the United States.

Kensington Park was created at a point just north of Grand River Avenue toward Milford. A dam was built across the river which raised the water level and created two lakes. In addition, the park contained three beaches, the two lakes, and fishing and hunting in the backwoods, and it became the week-end resort of thousands of families.

When Trendle's term expired, two of the commissioners so valued his services on the board that they personally went to the governor and asked that he be kept on the board. The governor promised the reappointment and asked that Trendle stay on until the formal appointment be made. After a few weeks of serving without a formal appointment, a fellow commissioner telephoned the governor's office and was told the paper would be sent to him "in a few days." Shortly thereafter Trendle received a telephone call from the manager of Huron Clinton Authority stating that a woman member of the U.A.W. Board of Directors had been appointed "to fill the post formerly held by George W. Trendle." No letter ever came from the governor.

Still, Trendle was content with the job he had done, and he was ready, as usual, to go on to the next job!

XXVIII

TRENDLE STOOD UP AS HIS ASSOCIATE entered the room and shook hands. "He does look extraordinarily well," he thought.

"Good to have you back, Mr. King."

"It is so beautiful in the north woods at this time of year. It is beautiful up there at any time of year, I guess. I hated to come down to the city. But now that I'm here, I'm glad to see my friends, and you in particular, George."

"You are looking very well."

"I get a little tired now and then. I'm getting up in years."

"We all get a little tired, Mr. King."

King nodded. He looked around the office. Paneled in mahogany, well carpeted and furnished, and with an artist's concept of the great horse Silver on the wall behind Trendle's desk, it was quite a contrast to the first office in which he had seen the man Trendle. How well he remembered the young man, seated on a high stool in the office but not of it, as if he were in a position to know everything that went on in the office even if he didn't enter into it. He remembered him with the books—forever the books under his arm!

"We've come a long way, George."

Trendle waited.

"Now you're a rich man and so am I. A long, long way we've come."

"Mr. King, would you like to get out of the business? Really retire and stay up in your northern county?"

King hesitated. "No, I don't think so, just as long as I can have my vacations up there. We could go on just as we are."

No reply come at once, for Trendle was thinking, "Each vacation begins where the last one ends." Aloud he said, "We got out of the picture business at just the right time."

King nodded.

"I think this is the right time to get out of the radio station too."

King remonstrated, "I am satisfied, George. We can go on just as we are, can't we?"

"We could get a very nice profit on our investment in the station, Mr. King."

"What would you consider a good price?" King would not turn down a profit.

"About ten times what we paid?"

King showed his amazement. "We paid two hundred fifty thousand, George. Do you think you can get two million five hundred thousand?"

"I am pretty sure we could, Mr. King." Then, after waiting for King to recover, he went on, "Would you be agreeable to selling if we could get that price?"

"I would be, George–I certainly would be. As you say, there is a time to get in and a time to get out. Ten times an investment is the time to get out."

George laughed. "I have your permission, then, to start the negotiations?"

"Certainly, George. Go ahead, negotiate." Then, shaking his head, "I never dreamed it would pay off so well," and almost as an afterthought, "what about the shows? A separate deal on them?"

Trendle, who had made his decision long ago on that, said, "Of course separate! But we'll work that out when the station is being sold."

"Fine," said the man, and then, as he had said so many times before, "you go ahead, George."

In spite of the heartiness of his reply, Trendle felt that King was reluctant to leave radio and that perhaps, just perhaps, he had given his approval to sell only because he was sure there was no chance of getting the price that had been named. So he kidded. "If I can get more, Mr. King, shall I take it?"

King laughed. "Part of every cent that I get on my forty per cent over what the two and a half million would bring is yours, George." And again, "You go ahead. George, I leave it in your hands."

In 1943 the radio station was sold to the American Broadcasting Company for $3,650,000. All the shows were retained by the King-Trendle Broadcasting Company.

A deal was worked out under the terms of which King transferred his interest in the several radio shows to Trendle. Now the shows which Trendle created and produced were controlled by him.

At this time the stock had been apportioned 40 percent to King, 40 percent to Trendle, 10 percent to Howard O. Pierce and 10 percent to H. Allen Campbell. A new allocation of stock was worked out. Trendle kept 70 percent for himself, and the remaining shares were taken over by H. Allen Campbell and Raymond J. Meurer.

Pierce retired and moved to Fort Lauderdale, Florida. King and Trendle saw very little of each other after the sale. King's wife died, and after a time King remarried and moved to California, and George heard nothing from him until he received word of his death from King's daughter.

Pierce had left the company long before the sale of the station. "All of my experience and inspiration came from visual, colorful live entertainment, and radio does not appeal to me at all."

Pierce would have been sensational in color television, but that was still years away when he left Detroit. He went to Fort Lauderdale and gave of his talents in volunteer work in the community. He loved Fort Lauderdale, and Fort Lauderdale loved him.

When the Trendles were in Fort Lauderdale each year on their winter vacation, the two men, Pierce and Trendle, would often get together, and old experiences were sometimes discussed. Once they shared a "rerun" of what they called the "Blackfoot king's anointment" from the theatre days.

"Do you remember? We were putting on, from time to time, something in the way of extra attractions in addition to the picture shows, at the Madison Theatre. An advance man for a group of Blackfoot Indians, who were appearing in different cities sponsored by the Union Pacific Railroad, asked for a week at the Madison.

"We engaged the troupe–and then the necessary publicity had to be worked up.

" 'President Coolidge,' said the advance man, 'was adopted into the Blackfoot tribe. Do you know a prominent Detroiter who would be willing to be adopted?'

"At that time," recounts Pierce, "I didn't know the mayor, but I did know his secretary, Ross Schram. Ross and I had gone to school together. He agreed to talk to the mayor.

" 'The Mayor,' said Ross, 'is not noted for his patience.' And that was the understatement of the year.

"The morning of the affair came. The papers carried the story. All was set. The mayor was waiting.

"In filed the whole tribe–men, women, children, forming a large circle around the mayor's desk and going right into their dance with their own music accompaniment. The performance went on and on. The mayor's face got redder and redder, but he kept his cool and submitted to the crowning with a hatful of feathers.

"By that time I was looking for the quickest exit; and I vowed the next 'king' would be anointed without me. The pavement of Woodward Avenue felt mighty good under my feet."

XXIX

THE FORTIES WERE LUSH YEARS for George W. Trendle. Until 1943, when the radio station was sold, the business had been very profitable. Now, with no other larger interest, the radio shows became his prime interest. As he was fond of saying, "Six programs—right across the board—and national!" "In the same time slot" was an accomplishment which no other producer had equaled, and he was justly proud. The profit? "Well, enough," said Trendle.

It was the extra revenue from these shows which amazed even Trendle. Licensing proceeds from forty-three manufacturers, comic strips and books ran very high. Such names as Endicott Johnson, Pioneer Suspender, Parker Brothers, Louis Marx and Grossett and Dunlap headed the list, manufacturing clothing, games, toys, cutlery, school pencils, pens and bags, books, raincoats, musical instruments, candies, chains, badges, rings, buttons, molds—all with the insignia of a member of the cast of one of the shows. Leading the list were the Lone Ranger items. Raymond J. Meurer became legal authority in charge of contracts with licensees. It was a tough job, and Muerer did it well. "No one could do that job as well as Ray," said Trendle. "He combined business acumen with a personality which allowed for firmness, when necessary, without arousing antagonism."

Business in the forties was "great."

In Trendle's personal life there was contentment. George junior had gone into the Army in World War II, been assigned to the Quartermaster Corps, received a permanent injury to his right arm and been honorably discharged—but not before he had spent many months in Percy Jones Hospital.

In 1947, George junior married his first wifc, Ruth, a marriage that was destined to become dissolved in a few years. He was established in his own law practice and making his ability felt in the legal field in Detroit. His father was proud of him.

Mary K. was married too. She had been graduated from Rollins College in Winter Park, Florida, met Dwight Johnson there and married him. Shortly after the marriage they moved to San Diego, California.

There was happiness in Trendle's life all through the forties. Business was very good, and his family was settled in a good pattern. But there was sadness too.

All through the years he had kept to the habit of keeping in daily touch with his mother. Sometimes she called him, but more often he telephoned her. Now it was his sister Jen who called.

"George, I don't like the way Mother looks. Have you heard from Clara?"

He hurried to his sister's apartment, and he didn't like the change in his mother's appearance either. She had been failing rapidly, he thought. But as they visited she seemed to brighten. They laughed and joked until it was time for him to leave.

Within a few days Clara called him. His mother had fallen while getting out of the bathtub and had broken her leg. She was taken to Harper Hospital, where she was put in traction. George visited her every day. After the first week it seemed she was getting better. In any case she was well enough to talk and laugh with her son.

During all the years when he visited her, she never got used to the idea that her son was in the entertainment field. "When will you try to be a judge, George?" she would ask. Once he said, "Mother, I want to help the youngsters help themselves—I don't want to judge them or anyone." She didn't give up the idea of her son sitting on the bench in what, to her, was the height of success, the ultimate in serving one's fellow man.

That the entertainment business had kept her and the

family in comparative luxury all these years didn't occur to her. She was grateful, but still it took a good deal of explaining to help her realize that what he was doing, through the shows, was of greater and more far-reaching results than the bench would have furnished—unless, of course, he reached the Supreme Court! And that was not beyond the aspiration of a mother either. She was reconciled to the fact that her son was happy and an influence for good, and her face would light up when someone mentioned his name.

During the hospital stay they would go over old times—the days when the girls were all at home and the family was together.

To amuse her, he asked, "Mother, do you remember the suitcase in St. Louis?"

She nodded and laughed. "Ah, sure, George. I should have known better." She wrinkled her face in the old familiar gesture; but full of sedation, she soon fell asleep. And George stayed a while, remembering.

It was while he was a young man in St. Louis, living in a boardinghouse for young men, that his mother had come down on a surprise visit. During the day, while he was at work, she busied herself with going over his clothing, sewing on buttons, mending little catches, darning socks. Finally, searching for work, she went into the closet and opened a suitcase. Inside the suitcase were two bottles of whiskey, one half filled, medication of a suspicious nature, and a few items of clothing wrinkled and dirty. This was beyond understanding, for her son was a neat person. When George arrived home that night, he thought she had been crying. She was very quiet—didn't speak beyond the greeting.

"Mother, what's wrong?"

"George, I want you to come home."

"I will, Mother, as soon as I am sure that I can find a job in Detroit. But you know that."

"I don't want you to stay here any longer at all. I don't

know what has happened to you. You used to be a neat, clean boy."

George was shocked. "Mother!"

"I went into the closet and opened that suitcase."

"Why would you climb up on the shelf? Besides, the case is empty. My clothes are hung up in the closet."

"Not the one on the shelf–the one on the floor."

"Oh, Mother, you shouldn't have opened that. It isn't mine. One of the fellows was moving, and he left it here until he gets settled in his new place."

The mother laughed her relief and put her arms around the boy. "Oh, I know my boy. I should never have doubted you. But I still want you to come home, George." And he did return soon afterward.

George sat at his mother's bedside day after day, sometimes not talking at all. He would hold her hand when she lapsed into a heavy sleep. Over and over her prayers were in German: "Lieber Gott–Lieber Gott–"

After nine weeks she lapsed into her final sleep. And George felt an emptiness which in his life had no parallel. Death had come before to the family: his young brother, but George was himself too young to remember him; then his sister Minnie–he missed Minnie; his father, although that death had little effect on George, for the father had left his family long before his death. This was different–as if a part of himself had left with his mother.

He had his wife, his son and daughter and his two sisters, but here was the one person who had loved him, wrong or right. Her warmth, her comfort, her approval and her faith in him were qualities never to be replaced by anyone in his lifetime.

XXX

"WRITERS ARE AN ODD-BALL LOT," said Mickey Merrill, in a conversation about the old days of broadcasting. She was one of the writers on the staff of radio station WXYZ. Offices for the writing staff were located at the broadcasting station on East Jefferson in Detroit. Writing, producing, broadcasting and recording were all done at the Jefferson Avenue Building. The executive offices had long been in the Stroh (now Mutual) Building in Detroit.

The building was an old mansion which had been built by one of Detroit's first families, the Mendelsohns. It was bought and converted to accommodate the broadcasting but not altered enough to lose its character. The old balustrades were left untouched; the fireplaces, of which there were many, had hand-carved mantels. The huge foyer with the center staircase at the back of the room had stairs going up right and left from the landing, the same as when the building was a residence. Above the landing was a huge globe of light with a map of the world, and at the sides were paintings in brilliant color of Tonto, the Long Ranger and the Green Hornet.

The building had a dignified quality, and yet it was warm enough to encourage creativity. At the left of the foyer was the broadcasting room with the engineer's or sponsor's booth at one end, and beyond that, to the left, was a large windowed room containing most of the sound-effects equipment. Here stood a door in a frame mounted on a stand so that when the sound of a door slamming was called for, a real door was slammed. Two large long troughs of sand were mounted on stands. Inside were plumber's helpers–plungers–of various sizes. During the broadcasting of the horses' gallop, two young men stood at this stand and manipulated the plungers in proper tempo to simulate horses' hooves.

Before the days of recorded sound these two young men were responsible for the sound effects, which were "live" as were the broadcasts. Various sounds were produced by various means, and everyone offered advice.

At one time, during rehearsal, the sound of a body falling into water was needed for the story. A large tub was brought in, and the sound-effects men experimented. A hand slapped across the water brought "No good, too thin" from the director, Chuck Livingstone. "Try a newspaper"–then, "No, not good." Time after time various things were dropped, but the effect was not satisfying to the director. The testing went on.

"Fine, that's just right!" called Chuck. "Try that last one again." And everyone in the studio burst into laughter. The two young men had been indulging in some horseplay, and one had jostled the other. The man slipped and fell into the tub.

Directly over the broadcasting studio were the writers' offices. The number varied from two to ten, but Fran Striker was always the head writer and in charge of the staff.

Striker was a prodigious writer. It was said that the number of words he wrote each year equaled or exceeded the number of words in the Bible. In addition to the radio script which he wrote he also wrote a dozen or more books on the old West, based on the Lone Ranger theory. His death, by automobile accident on the Buffalo Road, was a blow and a decided loss to all who knew him.

With two to ten writers, there are two to ten different personalities. Few writers put in an eight-hour day writing. They write when the spirit moves them, or more likely, when the deadline is breathing hot down their necks. Consequently much of their work is done after hours, at home, and since they are expected to be at the office during office hours, the time is spent in various ways. Much horseplay goes on!

"All employes will wear jackets during the work hours" was one of the rules. Believing that men work best when they think well of themselves, George followed the rule himself. No one saw him in the office in his shirtsleeves. "No smoking during office hours" except in lounge areas. There was good reason for this rule. In every broadcast station there are reams of paper, many records and cans and cans of tape. A fire in this place meant the destruction of valuable equipment which would take weeks to replace and lack of work during the replacement.

If rules are made to be broken, this is nowhere more true than where creative writers are concerned. Coats hung on backs of chairs, cigarettes smoldered in ash trays.

"Here comes the Boss" would be the signal for coats to be quickly donned and cigarettes snubbed. The offices were quite orderly when Trendle walked through them. The writers' offices looked out on the parking lot, and it was always easy to spot the blue Cadillac. Fran Striker, probably too busy to notice, never mentioned the infraction of rules; and if the Boss suspected, he didn't mention it.

About this time a book by Harry Bennet purporting to be the true story of Henry Ford's life came out. It was titled *They Never Called Him Henry*. One morning, as Trendle entered the back door from the parking lot, he looked up to see the sign "They Never Called Him George," which some prankster had hung in the back entrance hall. As indeed, they never did! His employees liked and respected him, but no one ever called him George. He was always addressed as Mr. Trendle.

One malcontent in the writing division felt his dignity had been assailed in some way, so he quit and got a job in New York on one of the networks' writing staffs. His writing ability was so pronounced that when he heard the man was unhappy in the new job, Fran Striker wrote and asked him if he wanted to come back. He responded with a letter which outlined all the good things he missed at the station under Fran: the working conditions, the freedom to develop ideas, the fine leadership and help of Fran Striker, all of which in formation took a whole page. Turning the page, one would be sure of his acceptance with gratitude, but he closed the letter with this: "All of these fine things are true, but I wouldn't work in Detroit for a thousand dollars a day." The letter was passed around, and everyone enjoyed a good laugh except Trendle, who shrugged and said, "What a punch line! That's better writing than he ever did here."

Mickey Merrill was for some time the only woman writer on the staff. Striker had hired her and thought a good deal of her ability to write–so much so that after a week or two he put her in almost complete charge of the writing of the "Sergeant Preston of the Yukon" show. She was popular with all the staff at the studio from writers to technicians.

One day a sound-effects man called at her office. Dewey could imitate a dog's bark in a way very nearly perfect. Just as in a real dog's bark, there is a difference between the sounds of fear, warning and joy, and Dewey was able to mimic the sounds with accuracy for the broadcasts. With another sound-effects man, a dog fight was reproduced to perfection.

"Miss Merrill," he began, "I have a couple of grandchildren who know that I work on the show, but they have never heard my voice. They want to brag to their friends about me, but how can they brag about a grandfather who barks?"

"I can understand your problem, Mr. Dewey. I'll write you into the next show." And she did, giving him a paragraph or more. Rehearsal went off in a fine manner. Then came the live broadcast.

Dewey stood before the mike right behind the actor who spoke before him, his script in his hand, when his cue came up. He stepped up close to the microphone, opened his mouth —and not a sound came out. Dewey had frozen.

Paul Sutton, playing Sergeant Preston, recognized the situation and ad-libbed to cover Dewey's freeze.

Later, trying to help Dewey overcome his embarrassment, Miss Merrill said, "Never mind, Dewey—that happens sometimes. I'll write you in again sometime soon."

Dewey shook his head. "No, thank you, Miss Merrill, I'll guess I'll just stick to barking."

Sutton had a voice which carried with it a connotation of authority—righteous authority. It was exactly the kind of voice that George Trendle thought a lawman should have. "He did an excellent job of portraying the Sergeant," said Trendle. "He really took the job seriously." Then he went on, "I remember the time Paul had an operation for double hernia, during which time we all went out to his home to call on him. We had three weeks of the show ahead. I knew the writers could keep him silent for one or more broadcasts. I called him one morning and told him so. Then I asked him when he thought he could come back.

" 'I'd certainly like to come back, Mr. Trendle, but I'm still weak and still in my wheelchair. I don't see how I can get there.'

" 'Paul, we want you back. Let me see what I can work out.' "

In a few hours Trendle called him back. "Paul do you think you can work if I send a limousine for you?"

"If you could get me into it."

"He was too big to carry," Trendle related, "so we had a ramp built at Paul's house and another at the back of the studio. We got him to the studio in his wheelchair. Livingstone, noting he looked tired, asked Paul if he thought he could go through a broadcast.

" 'Just get that mike down here.' The microphone was brought down to his level, and he began to broadcast his lines from the wheelchair. In another five or ten minutes he either forgot or didn't like the position, because he stood up before the tall microphone and read the rest of his line standing there. We used the ramp a few more times, that's all," recounted Trendle.

Sutton was keenly conscious of this duty to his community as well, and he entered public-service work. There was a Red Cross series designed to recruit nurses, or blood for the blood bank, or hospital services or whatever was needed at the time. It was during World War II.

Paul offered to do the dramatic readings for the Red Cross programs and came to the studio, some fifty miles from his home, on Saturday mornings. Otherwise he would not have worked on Saturdays at all.

It was about this time, in the old days of radio, that the great horse Hi Yo Silver was making personal appearances with the Lone Ranger, Brace Beamer, in the interest of safety programs. It was a thrilling sight. The spirited white stallion with Beamer in full regalia entered the arena, raced twice around, stopped short and slammed down to allow the rider to dismount and give his prepared talk on safety. It was a beautiful spectacle–and when Trendle heard the rumor that Brace Beamer was calling the horse a killer horse, Trendle telephoned him at once.

"What's wrong with Silver, Brace?"

"I wouldn't want anyone else to ride him, Mr. Trendle."

"Can you handle him?"

"It's not easy. I can ride him but only in the ring."

"Let me see what I can do, Brace. I don't want to get rid of that beautiful animal."

"Mr. Trendle, please don't try to ride Silver." Brace was genuinely concerned.

The following Sunday morning Trendle went to the stable. "Bring out Silver," he told the groom. He mounted the horse, entered the ring. The horse took him around the ring like lightning, then suddenly reared up, slammed down and stopped short. For the first time since his early riding days Trendle felt fear. He knew that this horse might unseat him and he'd be injured, but he was determined to ride Silver. He had reasoned out a plan; he decided that the horse had been trained to do what he was doing: enter the ring, race twice around the ring counterclockwise, rear up and stop short in the center of the ring.

Trendle entered the ring and reined the horse hard to go clockwise. Silver was as gentle as a kitten. Trendle had no trouble stopping, starting and putting him through his paces. Silver had in fact been trained to appear vicious. If anyone expected to see his owner thrown, he was disappointed.

Silver, with Brace Beamer as the Lone Ranger, appeared later at many important meetings: the New York Horse Show, the Cattlemen's Show in Chicago, and others with national import. The only private appearance was done at the request of President Roosevelt to please his grandchildren. It was on the lawn of the White House; both grandchildren were avid admirers of the Lone Ranger. On the tenth anniversary of the broadcasts of "The Lone Ranger," Trendle received a poem from his old friend, Edgar A. Guest, written especially for Trendle:

Ten Years of "Hi Yo Silver," ten years of riding hard!
Ten years of pistol shooting and still alive, unscarred!
Ten years of horse and rider, of wagon pack and stage.
Ten years of desperados and still no sign of age!
Ten years of "Me-called Tonto," the masked man's faithful scout—
A thousand times they've shot him, but still he rides about.

Ten years of hooves a-gallup, with never a sign of drag–
Ten years of laryngitis for good old Mustang Mag.

Three nights a week, I've listened (His devotee am I!)
To hear the masked man giving his long familiar cry:
"Hi Yo Silver, there is danger. It's time to hit the trail!
Beyond the gulch they're waiting to rob the Western mail!"
Ten years of good old Silver's persistent chase of thieves
And still no sign of spavin, or bott, or gall or heaves.
Ten years of vice and virtue! Then years of war with sin!
That's fifteen hundred battles and every one a win!

But now to change the picture. Ten years of scenes like these:
"Turn off the radio, Willie, and come to supper, please!"
Ten years of youth excited, wide-eyed and tousled brow,
replying, "Just a minute, the Ranger's on right now!
He's shouting 'Hi Yo Silver, Away–There's danger grave!
They're holding up the stage-coach! There's gold we've got to save!' "
Still, as when he started, the boys on every street,
Would rather hear the Ranger, than sit them down to eat.

Oh, who would trace the glory of ten such golden years
Would find it all lived over in countless brave careers!
He'd find it in the jungles, the seven seas and skies,
For who sets high example sets that which never dies.
Who walks the paths of honor takes many a lad along–
For boys are quick to follow where leadership is strong
And though he may not see them–the Lone Ranger of the air–
His followers are legion at home and everywhere.

Hi Yo Lone Ranger–Phantom Rider! Ten years they've called him that–
Ten years of boots and saddle and spurs and broadbrimmed hat.

And yet whate'er his journey or what the peril known
This is the truth about him—he never rides alone!
That cry of Hi Yo Silver, "There's danger now! Away!"
Calls forth a bright-eyed army to share it come what may.
Whatever strength is needed and faith too strong to fall—
Ten million boys and over, ride with him down the trail.

The poem was signed "Edgar A. Guest" and dated January 23, 1943.

George received it with gratitude, happy with one particular line: "For who sets high example sets that which never dies."

His beloved Lone Ranger! How he wished that everyone could see as well as hear the Lone Ranger, tall, broad-shouldered, slim-hipped, astride the great white stallion Hi Yo Silver! Although he didn't know it then, he would soon have his chance, and the Ranger would be seen by all.

XXXI

MIRACULOUS AS RADIO SEEMED at its parturition—sound coming out of the air, music, drama—the next development in the entertainment field was at first considered fantastic. Now pictures as well as sound came over the air waves!

This was TELEVISION!

Born as early as 1925, when some still pictures were broadcast by radio, the new medium was dubbed too risky, too farfetched, to be taken seriously. Nevertheless, the braver souls tried it here and there. The medium was too expensive for the average sponsor and the coverage too sparse. There were few sets for its use as effective advertising. Still, if radio appealed to the ear-minded and television appealed to the eye-minded as well, the whole of the potential audience would be covered. The impact would be incalculable.

In the beginning all the television stations ran in the red. Here again George's sense of timing asserted itself, and he waited. It was not until the 1950's that he ventured into television.

The organization which he headed bought a small television station in Flint. Rather, when they bought it, it was a radio station, also running with a low profit level. Allen Campbell was successful in selling time on this station, and the station was doing quite well when the decision was made that it was time to try television. The only wave length available was an ultrahigh frequency, and almost no television sets were equipped to handle that. So Allen Campbell, with his usual finesse, set about to sell the television audience on adding the special equipment necessary to receive their station's broadcasts. He sold it to 30 per cent of the potential listening and viewing audience!

It was not enough, however, and when a Detroit corporation offered to buy the station, the owners accepted.

Trendle still felt that his Lone Ranger should be seen as well as heard. He and Allen Campbell went to the radio show's long-time sponsor, General Mills, with the proposition that the radio show be dropped from its program and television substituted. It took a bit of selling by both Trendle and Campbell, but they succeeded.

General Mills, it must be said, is aggressively modern and maintains a large research department as part of its setup. Raymond T. Meurer was brought up from Detroit to handle the contract.

To the surprise of everyone in the industry, General Mills agreed to finance the production of the television films, but the actual production was to be left entirely in the hands of the Lone Ranger, Inc., with Trendle in command. General Mills did not interfere in the writing, directing, casting or filming, but left it in Trendle's competent hands.

"The Lone Ranger" went on television September 15, 1949, and General Mills was so pleased with the results that 130 shows were made–all very profitable to producers and sponsors and all used by General Mills throughout the country, except for the Southeast, where Merita Baking was the sponsor.

Trendle was delighted with the profit, but most of all, he was happy in the spirit of pioneering which went with the production. Here again he excelled in his choice of employees. Jack Chertok was given the contract for producing and for submitting a cast for approval. Clayton Moore, out of many applicants, became the Lone Ranger. Jay Silverheels was Tonto. This casting was conceded even by competitors to be as near perfect as possible.

Charles D. Livingstone had done such a good job of directing the radio shows that Trendle sent him to Hollywood to learn the art of directing in television. But Livingstone did not like Hollywood, and shortly came back to Detroit and entered other employment. According to Trendle, Livingstone had done a fine job in Hollywood but was unwilling to adjust to the Hollywood style of living.

Nevertheless, the shows were very good. All went smoothly, and the results pleased both Chertok and Trendle, who supervised. Happy with the success of "The Lone Ranger" productions, Trendle now turned to the second show, "The Challenge of the Yukon," later renamed "Sergeant Preston of the Yukon."

This was a different story. The sponsor of the radio shows, Quaker Oats Company, were quite convinced of the merit of television advertising but said they had never financed a television production. It was difficult to convince them that the venture would be profitable. The shows were costing about $25,000 each to produce. Eventually Quaker Oats agreed to put up the money.

Jack Chertok was approached with an offer to produce the Yukon shows, but he was fully committed and could not handle another show. He offered, "Let me get a list of recommendations for you. I'll inquire around and see who's free."

A man named Charles Skinner was discussed. His references were very good, and he seemed a good choice. Trendle took the precaution of hiring a liaison man who would keep him informed and who would if necessary act as a buffer between him and the parties concerned. The liaison man was Freddie Fralick, an old friend. He kept Trendle fully posted on what was going on out there and offered some valuable suggestions as well. The two men became friends.

About two hundred names were offered by the casting department to fill the part of Sergeant Preston. The list was reduced to eighty and later to twelve. These twelve were put in the rented Mounty costumes, wearing pasted-on false mustaches, and required to ride the black horse which had been rented from a local studio.

Dick Simmons looked the part of Sergeant Preston, as Trendle had conceived him. He was chosen to star in the pictures. A couple of weeks later the entire company was sent up into the hills near Aspen, Colorado, to shoot the first pictures.

For the first hour all went well. Then, suddenly, Dick Simmons was on the ground, groaning and vowing that nothing would induce him to ride that black horse again. Whether the horse had tripped on the rough ground or acted in some way to cause Simmons to leave the saddle, no one seemed to know.

Trendle was notified by telephone and went immediately to the shooting location.

"Doctor, is he badly hurt?"

"He's all right, Mr. Trendle. I'll need X rays, of course, but I think we'll find nothing more than a broken wrist."

"That's bad enough," said Trendle.

"It is sometimes painful, but we'll apply a cast. He should be entirely well in about one month."

"Do you think you can disguise the cast? Can't you hide it under his coat and have him go on anyway?"

"He couldn't ride–and he'd be very clumsy. The cast has to go down over his hand."

Trendle talked to Freddie Fralick, who had called him, and said, "We'll have to forget the horse I bought for a while, Fred. Get rid of the horse; he's apparently too frisky for this type of job. Just rent a studio horse."

For once Trendle was depressed. Obstacles usually stimulated him, but this development was topping most of the other obstacles. Unhappy with the appearance of the rented horse, Trendle decided to change the show completely to a winter show and dog sleds.

"Freddie, what do you know about Eskimo sled dogs?"

"There is a man in Colorado who raises them. Will you go?"

"By the next train." George left for Colorado, and found it hard to choose from so many fine dogs but eventually made his choice. Yukon King was as fine a specimen as could be imagined. When the other dogs were chosen for the dog sled, King was "free lead" as if he had been born to it, as he really was, and he kept the dogs in line. King was valuable to the show, but in one of the scenes King broke a toe and had to be immobilized. An understudy took over.

"All right," called the director. "Get in the water." The star got into the cold water of the Colorado rivulet and splashed around as if he were drowning.

"Get that dog in there!" the director shouted. "He has to do the rescue scene!"

The understudy was pushed, out of camera range, toward the water. He entered the cold stream, but as soon as the cold water hit his haunches, he howled and darted out of the water.

"Once more," said the director, losing patience, and once more the dog howled and darted back out of the water.

"Get another understudy." And a dog less temperamental went into the water.

Another time the stand-in for the injured King was called upon to rescue his master from a burning cabin. At the risk of disappointing the viewing public, it can be told. The illusion of a burning building is created by placing an inflammable substance in a narrow trough around the spot where the action is to take place. Just before the cameras roll, the substance is lighted.

The Sergeant was lying inside the ring, the fire was lighted, and the understudy was sent in to drag out his master. Unfortunately he ran too close to the fiery trough, singed his rear and broke out of the ring howling. A wiener was attached to a string and dragged through the ring. Most dogs fell for this old trick, but this dog ran a short way and came back howling again. Again the understudy for the understudy was employed!

"Get rid of that dumb dog!" yelled the director.

But Trendle's love of animals prevailed. He pointed out the fine qualities of the dog, his superior appearance, his genuine intelligence. Human stars employ some tactics too. "Keep the stand-in–he'll be handy."

The exterior shots were made in the snow around Aspen, and the background was authentic, It was beautiful, but the weather there was tricky. With forty actors on location in Colorado, eating up the operating expense, there were ten days of weather too cloudy to shoot pictures.

"Freddie," said Trendle, "I can see the whole operation going down the drain. Here we have made four pictures instead of seven, and we're in the red $126,000. The budget for seven pictures has been used up."

"Will Quaker Oats go for an extra amount?"

"No, I couldn't go to them for more money. They'd lose faith in our ability to make pictures according to our agreement. We might lose the client entirely."

"Well, you can't risk that."

"No, but something has to be done at once."

"I'm not happy with the situation, Freddie. What do you think?" But the man would not commit himself. "Do you have any other ideas, George?"

After many conferences Skinner resigned, and Trendle put Tom Curtis in charge. Later he said, "Tom Curtis was just what the doctor ordered." A studio in Hollywood was rented. A brand-new Arctic scene was built, and used for fifty pictures. Tom Curtis really was doing a good job!

Trendle went to the National Bank of Detroit and borrowed enough to cover the losses. With the new setup, the loss was offset, and the show made money for both the owners and the sponsor. The tax on corporations' profit at that time was about 50 per cent, so approximately 50 per cent of the loss was paid indirectly by the government.

Almost as important as the money involved was the faith that was restored to Trendle. He had had phenomenal luck in choosing the right man for the right job previously, and to have chosen the wrong one this time was almost unthinkable. Tom Curtis, having been studio manager for Metro-Goldwyn-Mayer, was tailor-made for the job of producing the Yukon shows. Fralick, Curtis and Chertok all remained loyal to Trendle throughout the years. And someone said, "This kind of loyalty is most unusual in Hollywood–or in any other place in the picture business."

XXXII

Back in the old theatre days Trendle was in New York on a business trip when Sam Goldwyn got in touch and asked him, "What would you take as a salary to work in Hollywood with our firm?"

George answered in a split second. "I do appreciate your offer, Mr. Goldwyn, but there isn't enough money minted to make me move out there. My home, my friends and family, are in Michigan. That's home! I have never even thought about leaving for any reason. No, but thank you very much."

It was true; George loved his home. But now he found himself spending every fifth week in California. He still went over every single script to be sure the shows were up to the standards he had laid down. Every fifth week he was shown the rushes of film for the television productions. It was action —he liked it!

About seven one morning he thought someone was shaking him.

"Yes, yes—what?—what?" he mumbled in his sleep. Then he opened his eyes, looked at his watch and wondered if he weren't dreaming. The hotel room was on the eighth floor of the Beverly Wilshire Hotel, facing a large swimming pool. He looked out the window and saw the water in the pool sloshing from side to side as if someone were tipping it to spill the water out. Soon, as he watched, it was empty. Trendle went back to bed.

"I don't know what it is—but I know something is definitely wrong," he said to himself. The bed was jiggling so that he couldn't get back to sleep. He got out of bed, dressed completely, including his hat, and walked to the elevator. By this time the building was shaking so that he had to hold onto the walls.

The night watchman was running the elevator. He looked surprised to see Trendle. "I thought everyone was out of this floor."

"Why, what's going on?"

"Don't you know? We're having an earthquake or a series of them."

"Start this thing and get me down," and the elevator started down.

Assembled in the street in various degrees of undress were the hotel guests, employees, management–in negligees, nightgowns, pajamas, bathrobes. George was the only person fully clothed.

A well-known comedian, guest of the hotel, called out, "Hey, George, did you just get in? Then what in hell are you doing with all those clothes on?"

"If this place falls down, and I have to go elsewhere, I'd rather not travel in my bathrobe."

"I'll get back in and get dressed, too," one of the guests said, still dazed from fright.

"Better not," said George. "I think it might be wise to go across the street away from this wall. It could fall in, you know."

The whole group started across the street, and when they were about halfway across, another quake shook the earth. It was more than an hour later that the group felt safe enough to go back into the building. Later Trendle learned it was a "number seven" earthquake and regarded as quite serious.

After that Trendle would specify, when making reservations, "Not above the fourth floor," thereby mystifying the hotel clerk. But if he had to be away from home, he wanted no worries. He remembered old worries.

It was just before television, one day, that the office telephone rang. "Mr. Trendle, the horse is sick." Trendle was genuinely concerned. It seemed impossible that this beautiful animal, the first Hi Yo Silver to make the Lone Ranger appearances, should succumb to ailments of ordinary horses. A day of investigation with various veterinarians made Trendle even more unhappy. He sent the horse to Lansing to the university veterinarian.

"The horse is too sick, Mr. Trendle; he cannot get well. It would be a kindness to put him to sleep."

Reluctantly Trendle agreed, and asked for an autopsy. He arranged for a cremation and stayed on until that too was over.

Then began the search for a replacement. A Dr. Hudson, veterinarian at Michigan State University, said that he knew of a horse at Colorado Springs so nearly like Hi Yo Silver that no one would know the difference. Trendle took the train to Colorado and examined the horse. He seemed to have conformation very similar to that of Hi Yo Silver. He was seemingly pure white, but Trendle noticed some light tan splotches on the horse's hips.

"Just stable stains," said the owner. "This horse is pure white."

The horse was purchased and shipped to the stable of Hi Yo Silver. "Wash him," the groom was instructed.

In a few moments, "Mr. Trendle," cried the groom, "come here quickly, please!" Under the horse white paint mixed with oil, chalk and other white substances was running down from the horse's two sides. Going down the drain with it, Trendle saw the $1,500 he had paid for this brown and white horse!

Trendle, who was scrupulously honest in his dealings, was furious. He called the former owner to account. The fellow laughed and said, "Well, that's horse trading for you, Mr. Trendle."

"I'll sue you for everything you have," was the response.

"I don't think so, Mr. Trendle. You'd be the laughing stock of the industry, and it wouldn't do your show, 'The Lone Ranger,' any good either."

This statement startled Trendle. The realization that the man was right hit him like a mallet. He would never do anything to harm that show, so he accepted the loss. He found another horse in Palm Springs, California–a pure-white animal, the very image of the first Lone Ranger's Hi Yo Silver. The tan-splotched horse was accepted in trade. The trade-in value of the tan-splotched horse was only $500, while the new Hi Yo Silver cost a good deal more, but still the allowance was appreciated by Trendle

Years later he would refer to the incident as "my lesson in horse trading."

XXXIII

"When will the Green Hornet go on TV, Mr. Trendle?"

"What about the Green Hornet, Mr. Trendle?"

"The Lone Ranger and the Sergeant Preston shows are doing so very well, how about the Green Hornet for TV?"

Over and over Trendle was asked the same question: What about the Hornet on TV? But the good news that the other two shows were doing so well prompted him to leave well enough alone.

Of the Ranger, 130 TV episodes had been made—all good! General Mills, true to their word, had offered no interference whatever, and the profit was very nice to contemplate.

With the new director, the Yukon pictures were doing well too. And Trendle was tempted, for it was contrary to his nature to rest on his laurels. He began to plan. His first obstacle was lack of time. He already had as much as any person could properly handle. Still there was the challenge.

"The Green Hornet" had gone on the air for the first time on January 10, 1936—radio, that is—sustaining on the twelve stations of the Michigan Radio network. On November 10, 1936, it was sponsored by the Detroit Ebling Company. In June, 1938, it went on the Mutual Network.

A young newspaperman named Clifford Prevost had access to City Hall news through his regular newspaper job. He suggested to George that this City Hall news be included in the Green Hornet show. But George refused; he felt it would confuse the real with the unreal and give a false impression to the listener. However, he did like the idea of fresh political news, and he hired Cliff to do a separate program. It was called "Town Talk," and in order to keep it entirely without bias, it had no sponsor. It earned a large audience on Saturday nights. It was strictly a public-service show! And it stayed that way, never being tied in any way to the Green Hornet.

"The Green Hornet," on March 15, 1940, was a top-rated show, according to the Crosley Rating Service. At that time it was unsponsored, but National Broadcasting Company kept it on the air until August, and then it went to Mutual Broadcasting, until October. Off the air in October, it went back on in June, sponsored by Orange Crush twice a week. In 1952 it went off the air permanently.

In 1963 a letter came from a Hollywood museum requesting placement of two Green Hornet displays in the American Legion display in that museum "to foster and perpetuate the motion picture, radio, recording and television industry.

Requests from Australia, South America and Canada for "The Green Hornet" came in. It was sponsored in those places at various times. In the United States the shows had been made on record and on tape. As in the Lone Ranger operation, the Green Hornet had comic books, premiums and so forth which proved quite popular at the time.

"Was the Green Hornet a neglected child of the publicity department?" Trendle was asked.

"I don't know–it's possible. We were very busy with the other shows, and it is natural to have the popular child get more attention, even at home."

While in Hollywood, he had a call from Las Vegas. "It is someone calling you for Steve Lawrence," he was told. Steve Lawrence and Eydie Gorme were two of Trendle's favorite performers. He took the call.

"Would you be interested in selling 'The Green Hornet'?" the voice at the other end of the line asked.

"Can you come to Detroit?" Trendle inquired.

"No, we have commitments here. Could you possibly stop here on your way to Detroit?"

At dinner in Las Vegas, on his way home, Trendle talked the deal over with the Lawrences. Nothing came of it. Perhaps the Lawrences did not want to increase their holdings and responsibilities at that time. More than likely, however, it was George Trendle himself who stalled on the deal. He had a special feeling for "The Hornet." "This is a show that could last forever," he said. "This show is based on modern-day problems and it can be changed to fit the times." It is entirely possible that he may not have tried to sell it to the Lawrences.

The question persisted, "Mr. Trendle, will 'The Green Hornet' go on television?"

With two shows being televised under his direct supervision, Trendle went to Hollywood once every four weeks, correcting and revising script and holding critiques after the rushes. It would have been impossible for him to do anything more and do it in the efficient manner which he demanded of himself.

In 1966, however, the American Broadcasting Company bought the right to make and market twenty-six television motion pictures starring the Green Hornet and using the Green Hornet formula. So well satisfied were they with the success of the radio program that they did not request a pilot for its use in television. Twentieth-Century-Fox's Greenway Productions were to do the filming, paying Green Hornet, Inc., for services plus royalties. The agreement was that George W. Trendle was to approve script and cast.

At once the question came to Trendle, "Since Greenway films 'Batman,' will the Green Hornet develop into a way-out character?"

"Absolutely not, if I can prevent it." Patiently he explained, " 'The Green Hornet' is based on real-life situations. The only fantasy is in the dealing with the villain–the fast car, the ray gun, and the anonymity of the hero. I don't want cat women, penguins or jokers."

George went to the Coast to choose the cast. Van Williams,

a handsome, well-built young man, a fine actor and intelligent, was chosen to play Britt Reid, the Green Hornet. The excellent choice lent credence to the part. However, when the first films were shown, it was evident that the story was being interpreted in a far different manner from what had been intended by Trendle. Although they were sticking to the main story in the script, there had been added disappearing staircases, an apparatus for icing the street to discourage followers, and other equally fantastic gadgets.

Trendle was dismayed. Ideas introduced into the production of the film were very displeasing to him. He felt that the television film bore little resemblance to the radio show which had been so popular.

"The Green Hornet," like its theme song, "The Flight of the Bumblebee," faded out of television but not out of the minds of the owners.

"There is a place for this type of hero in everyday life in every generation," said Trendle. "I am convinced that sooner or later some wide-awake advertiser will be interested in sponsoring a television series of the Green Hornet made according to the original concept. I am confident it will be a great success."

While he was on vacation in Florida with Mrs. Trendle, in March, 1952, he heard rumors that the Jack Wrather organization was interested in buying "The Lone Ranger." He waited, but no direct offer came. He telephoned Allen Campbell, who was also vacationing in Florida at the time.

"Allen, I read in the *Sun-Sentinel* that the Wrather staff are here on convention."

Wrather, an oil millionaire from Texas, felt an affinity with the Lone Ranger. He had admired the way the show was handled. The Lone Ranger was supposed to be a Texan–a perfect combination for Wrather, romance, and profit too.

Allen called Trendle. "What do you think of our going over to meet Mr. Wrather? He has asked to see us. But are you sure, Mr. Trendle, that you want to part with the Ranger?"

"Allen, I'm pushing seventy now, and I'm not going to tell you from which side I'm pushing."

Allen laughed.

Trendle said, "I'd like to divest myself of responsibility. I'd like to leave my estate in a more liquid form. As things are now, the whole thing could be tied up for years if anything happened to me." He thought for a moment; then he said, "You are right, I'd miss the Ranger."

"Shall we go over to Miami to meet Wrather?"

"Get an appointment; we'll go."

Nothing was decided then, but in the fall of 1952, Jack Wrather, accompanied by a business associate and his tax attorney, came to Detroit and arrived at George's office. It was settled that he wanted to buy, and the dickering over price began. It was a game both men, Wrather and Trendle, played to perfection, and they entered into the negotiations with zest.

Finally they arrived at the price except for a difference of $25,000. It looked like a genuine stymie to the others in the room, but the negotiators knew differently.

George turned to Allen Campbell. "Do you have a half dollar?"

"Yes–why?" said Allen as he handed the coin to George.

George turned to Wrather. "I don't want to drop a deal of this size for the sake of twenty-five thousand dollars. If you're game, I'll flip this coin to decide whether you pay the difference or not."

Wrather laughed. "You, Mr. Trendle–everyone knows that you don't gamble." In a moment he said, "Wait–we'll talk this over."

He went into a huddle with his associate and his tax attorney while Trendle and his associates huddled. "I'll eat my hat if he takes this one," said Campbell.

Wrather finally said, "Mr. Trendle, I know you don't

usually gamble and I suggest that now gambling would have no point. Suppose we just split the difference."

The deal was completed and "The Lone Ranger"—television, radio, comics and contracts for gimmicks all in a neat bundle—was transferred to the new owners, the Jack Wrather Enterprises.

"What a day!" said Allen Campbell on the way out.

"Quite a day," said Ray Meurer.

"I need just one thing to make it complete," said Trendle.

Together the men asked, "What is that?"

"We got all but twelve thousand five hundred dollars of the price asked, and that's pretty good." George grinned.

"What more do you want?" asked Campbell.

"Back there when we were negotiating, you said you'd eat your hat if we got a higher price. Now, let's see you take a bite."

Campbell laughed. "I didn't wear one today. I thought I'd better not."

Trendle quoted scripture: "O ye of little faith." The three men laughed together, as they had so often before.

Wrather proved a fine new owner. His statement for the press after the sale amounted to the credo, almost word for word, that had been laid down for the Lone Ranger by Trendle:

"The Lone Ranger is a composite of every man who stands for law and order, always stresses the fact that the young people of America owe much to their ancestors. To pay this debt, they must maintain their heritage and pass it on to their own descendants. All of these things teach something. They teach patriotism, fairness, tolerance, sympathy, religion. Yet, they don't preach. These lessons, once learned can never be forgotten."

And George, reading this, said, "The Lone Ranger is in good hands."

XXXIV

ALLEN CAMPBELL WAS BLESSED with a personality which inspired trust and respect, prime ingredients for sales ability. Now he sat in Trendle's office exchanging banalities, when suddenly he said, "Mr. Trendle, there is a pretty good little station in Pontiac which is going begging for good management."

"Allen, what's on your mind?"

"I think you and I could make a go of it, Mr. Trendle, if we bought it now."

"I don't want to go to Pontiac every day—or be responsible for a job which I know you could do very well without me."

"I am willing to do the active management, but I'd really like to have you in with me on this."

"I have always enjoyed working with you, Allen, and if you are confident this will work out, I am pretty sure that it will."

"Then you'll come in?"

"As treasurer, Allen. You would be president."

Thus the two friends entered upon a partnership. With mutual respect and understanding, they worked together for another six years.

But the station was in Pontiac, and Trendle's interests in Detroit also demanded time. When Campbell intimated one day that he might be interested in buying Trendle's stock, his offer was accepted, and the two men parted the best of friends.

The six years' interest in the Pontiac station had been profitable under Allen Campbell's management. and Trendle was pleased with the entire deal.

"And now," as radio and television announcers are wont to say, this biography will come to its close. It may seem to end abruptly, but that is because it has not really ended at all.

George Washington Trendle is alive and well at this moment in 1971. He maintains regular business hours, going to his office every day, including Saturdays, just as he has every week of his working life.

He lost the last remaining member of his immediate family in 1969 when his sister Clara died. Jen had preceded her by several years and Min many years before that. Mother, father and brother too had gone on, and George Trendle realized a sense of desolation he had never realized before. He was the last of his family. It was a very lonely feeling.

Friends too had gone. Fran Striker, brilliant writer and head of the writing staff at WXYZ, died in an automobile accident near his home in Buffalo, where he had gone from Detroit.

Brace Beamer, who had played the Lone Ranger through much of the radio days, died in Oxford, Michigan. This was a loss to all of those who shared the microphone with him, hand cupped over one ear, while the other hand held the sheaf of papers known as script.

Paul Sutton, who gave of his talent in interpreting that keeper of law and order in the great Northwest through his Sergeant Preston role, died in 1970. He had never been known to refuse his services to any good cause; his life was filled with service to his fellow man, and his loss was a particularly painful one to George Trendle.

There were other losses, but it was not in the nature of Trendle to luxuriate in self-sympathy or to lose himself in grief. He turned as usual to work. "When you work, you are a flute through whose heart the whispering of the hours turns to music." If he knew these lines of Kahlil Gibran, he didn't repeat them, but he lived them nevertheless.

Into his office letters continued to pour, many of them still to "The Lone Ranger." Every one of these was answered, with "Ta-i Ke-mo Sah-be" ("Greetings, Trusty Scout").

Letters still come in for the Green Hornet. So realistic was this hero pictured that letters asking him for help to "clean up the political situation in our town" still come. Every one of these is answered.

Trendle keeps in touch with his family. His daughter Mary K. in California, recently widowed, has as her prime concern her four children. They are Mary K. Johnston, recently graduated from college; William Trendle Johnston, just out of high school; young George Johnston, ready to enter high school; and Ann, the youngest of the family. Their grandfather values the mail which brings letters from them.

His son, George Washington, Jr., has left Detroit with his family–his wife and two daughters–to settle in Hawaii. Perhaps he has inherited the pioneering spirit of his father, and that prompted his move to our newest state. He writes regularly.

All of this is family correspondence. There is more of the business kind, though. Some time ago Trendle became interested in the newest entertainment in the electronics field. Now he plays with the idea of making cassette tapes of his shows.

If one approaches the office of George W. Trendle with the expectation of hearing a Lone Ranger close, "Hi Yo Silver–Away," then the question "Who was that man?" and hoof beats receding into the distance, and the answer "Why, that was the Lone Ranger," one would be in for a surprise. For there is no indication of the show's close here.

The creator of the Lone Ranger maintains regular business hours, including Saturdays. His time is taken up with many facets of work–his investments, his contracts with agents, and most of all, the future of his many remaining shows.

One hundred taped shows of "The American Agent"—this show of the American newspaperman who functions for his government in the capitals of Europe—are in the broadcasting future. In the back of Trendle's mind is the plot for another spy series, this one with a war background.

"The Green Hornet," his first love in importance, not in time, is still broadcast occasionally, and he has plans for a return to its former popularity. Trendle is always willing to talk about the Green Hornet. When he does, one feels a restlessness within the man. He goes on, "If the Federal Communications Commission changes its policy and conditions are such that an independent writer or producer can bring out his own shows as I did, I'd be more than delighted to do it all over again."

Again, one feels that he is lonely for the companionship of his former associates. If the shows which he controls could be offered directly to the sponsors, he would gather the remnants of his past organization and make a bid for television time.

"It is just as good today, in any locality, as it was the day it began. Designed to reach the young adult, it is hoped to give him an awareness of the need for watchfulness in the politics of his own city; to show there is always the possibility of error, intentional or not, in the politics of today. And it is the duty of every individual to seek out and correct these errors.

"These young people are in a better position than ever to bring about improvement in our government. I have great faith in the youth of today."

Here, then, was the dedication of his own life: "something for the young people of America." He gave them "The Lone Ranger," "The Challenge of the Yukon," "The American Agent" and "The Green Hornet," all with the single purpose to "create citizens and leaders with integrity and purpose."

And then the question came, "Mr. Trendle, which of the days of your active career do you consider the most important, the most exciting?"

He stood very still for a moment, and in his fine, firm voice gave the answer, "Tomorrow."

A925